surfgirl's
guide to
surfing

the essential guide for surf chicks everywhere!

Simon Williams

PUBLISHED BY ORCA PUBLICATIONS LTD

ISBN 0-9523646-4-3

surfgirl's
guide to
surfing

The essential guide for surf chicks everywhere!

Mary Bagalso Simon Williams

contents

COVER PHOTO: Sam Cornish. Photo: Courtesy Roxy.

CHELS

reef®

EA GEORGESON

ATURED PRODUCT THE ZEN

REEF.COM

REEF UK T: +44 (0)1243 673666 E: JON@THEWATERSPORTS.CO.UK

ROBYN DAVIES
British Nationals Women's Champion 2003

O'NEILL
ONEILLEUROPE.COM

Why we surf

Why do we surf? What inspires us? Is it to harness the power of the ocean or be at one with it? To take on the guys or check out the guys? Because it looks cool? Because our friends are doing it? Surfer and writer Rebecca Heller explains why it's the best sport in the world.

I think different people have different reasons for surfing. What I know is that when you are surfing it feels like you are flying, you are a part of nature, and it feeds your soul. Surfers get a bad rap because when we talk about surfing our eyes glaze over and we slip into some other part of our brain that seems a little sun-baked, when really we are just thinking about our last ride or our next one. You might think we're taking it all a little too seriously, but it happened to me and I can see it in other people's eyes. Once you stand up on your first wave you're done for. All you can think about is the next time you're going to get out in the water. You start getting up and going to bed early. You spend all your time at the beach. You've got "surf stoke." It's the best kind of drug there is — it's free and has no harmful side effects.

The great thing about surfing is that you don't need to be a professional or on a team to participate. There's no competition. All you have to do is play. The person having the most fun is always the winner whether they can stand up or not.

And being a girl in the water has its benefits. Girls, as opposed our more machismo counterparts, are actually out there to have fun. There is often a group of stunned guys trying to look tough and horde waves as girls socialise with their friends and cheer each other on. I love paddling out near some guy who I can tell is thinking, "Oh great, here comes another BLUE CRUSH-inspired girl thinking she can surf," passing him by as I point my board towards shore and getting a perfect ride. Around that time the guys either sit there a little dumbstruck, decide to ignore you or, better yet, try to talk to you.

As you may very well know, surfing is not easy. You can't expect to just pick up a board, head out to the beach and shred. Just like other sports it takes a lot of practice to become skilled. What makes surfing harder than other sports is you are on a constantly changing canvas. Surfing blends a rare combination of athleticism and grace usually reserved for figure skaters and ballerinas. Watching great surfers (professional or soul) is like watching a distilled dance of man and water, of a person at one with nature. Catching the perfect wave, being in just the right spot at just the right moment and taking the ride feels, I imagine, like hitting a hole-in-one or scoring at Old Trafford on a Saturday afternoon. One moment of sheer perfection. And even when your arms are weary, you paddle back out in the hope of catching another.

The sport of surfing is only half of it. Check out our playground! I have surfed reefbreaks where bright blue and yellow fish swam below and beachbreaks where dolphins, (which you could swear were trained at Sea World) jumped and dived in the waves. There is something that just feels so right about floating over a rhythmic sea. Something peaceful. Getting tumbled is only Mother Nature's awesome power reminding you that while she may let you charm her, she can certainly never be conquered.

Why do we surf? You will have to answer that question for yourself, but I'll tell you one thing, a parking lot filled with gorgeous guys changing under their towels doesn't hurt.

Grab a board, go out there and get wet!

Photo: Simon Williams

Contributors

 Tracy Boxall a former British Champion, is one of the UK's leading girls surf instructors and has coached the Junior World teams. She runs her own surf school in Wales.

South African born Kay Holt is the current British Professional Champion. She lives in Newquay working as a teacher. She grew up surfing the powerful breaks in South Africa.

 Lauren McCrossan is a full-time author and freelance writer. She divides her time between her home in Southwest France, Ireland, the UK and Hawaii. She is married to pro surfer Gabe Davies.

Steve England is one of the UK's most respected surf authorities. He is the assistant editor of Carve and SurfGirl magazines and has worked as a surf coach and lifeguard.

Ester Spears is a freelance photographer, writer and British coach. He lives in Croyde in North Devon.

Rowena Wilson works as a freelance writer, musician and teacher which enables her to get plenty of wave action. She lives in Brighton.

Jacqueline Wild is a writer and artist with a love of the land and the ocean. She surfs in Penwith and her local break is Sennen.

 Dominique Munroe is one of Britain's best female longboarders and surf instructors. She currently runs a Surf Academy for girls in St Agnes with Sarah Bentley.

PUBLISHING DIRECTORS
Steve England   Louise Searle

EDITORIAL CONSULTANT
Chris Power

DESIGN
David Alcock

PRODUCTION
Mike Searle

AD SALES
Steve England

EDITORIAL CONTRIBUTORS
Tracy Boxall Kay Holt Sarah Bentley Dominique Kent Lauren McCrossan Ester Spears
Jacqueline Wild Rowena Wilson Rob Barber Rebecca Heller

PHOTOGRAPHIC CONTRIBUTORS
Estpix Tim McKenna Simon Williams Mike Searle Chris Power Joli Tara Moller Pete Frieden John Callahan Cheryl Davies

SurfGirl's Guide to Surfing is published by Orca Publications Ltd, Berry Road Studios, Berry Road, Newquay, Cornwall TR7 1AT. Tel: 01637 878074 Email: info@orcasurf.co.uk Website: www.surfgirlmag.com

Colour repro: PH Media 01726 69924. Printed by Pensord, Blackwood, Wales.

KEALA

billabong

Keala Kennelly
Pic PAUL NAUDE
billabonggirl.com

Preparing for takeoff

The key to surfing is understanding the rhythm of nature by assessing situations, observing the ebbs and flows of tidal swell and learning from those with more experience. The sooner you do all three, the quicker you'll progress.

knowledge is gained by learning

Thomas Szasz, theorist

Types of waves

Ocean waves are some of
the most complicated
phenomena on earth.
However, you don't need to
become an oceanographer to
understand the basics of how
they're formed, and how they break.

Waves come in all shapes and sizes but the majority
of them are produced the same way, by winds blowing
across the oceans and creating swells. (The exceptions are
tsunamis which are caused by submarine earthquakes, and tidal
waves such as the Severn Bore.)

The best type of swells for surfing are groundswells, which are
generated many hundreds of miles away by winds revolving around distant
low pressure systems. Classic surfing conditions occur when a solid groundswell
combines with an offshore wind. Lines of waves can be seen stacked up way out to
sea, and the waves themselves are smooth and a joy to ride.

Well-organised groundswells are made up of 'trains' of waves, some of which are slightly
out of synch with the others. When the crests of two wave trains synchronise, the result is a group
of larger waves called a 'set'. Experienced surfers sit and wait for these sets, which arrive at regular
intervals, because they're always the biggest and best waves.

When a low pressure system passes close to the shore it brings stormy, wet weather and a different type of
swell called a windswell. Windswell waves can be just as big as groundswell waves but they're choppy, disorganised,
and tend to back-off a lot... in other words they're not much fun to ride.

When open-ocean swells move into shallower water they decelerate, 'feel' the seabed, and eventually break as waves.
The manner in which waves break depends largely on the configuration of the seabed.

Callaghan

Surfers use three classifications to describe the main different types of surfbreak.

Beachbreaks

SCANAIR

FISTRAL: A CLASSIC BEACHBREAK SETUP.

Beachbreaks, such as Fistral Beach in Cornwall, are the best place for beginners to learn to surf as the waves tend to be slowish and they break over sand. The peaks at a beachbreak will move around from one week to another as the sandbars below shift with the currents.

Pointbreaks

ESTPIX

CORDUROY LINES WRAP AROUND A LEFT HAND POINT

Pointbreaks, like Lynmouth in Devon, are rocky headlands around which waves peel (either to the left or right). Good pointbreaks provide long, racy waves which 'wall up' as you ride along them. They're not suitable for beginners (because of rocks and rip currents), but are generally okay for competent intermediates.

Reefbreaks

Mike Searle

THE PEAK IN ALL ITS GLORY

Reefbreaks, like The Peak at Bundoran in Ireland, are the most demanding breaks of all, and should only be tackled by advanced surfers. These are spots where waves break straight onto shallow ledges of rock. If conditions are perfect, a reefbreak will sometimes provide barrelling waves as the lip of the breaking waves pitches and throws out to form a

A few of the very best pointbreaks and reefbreaks in Britain and Ireland are referred to as 'secret spots' in surfing lore. These are places the local surfers and bodyboarders don't want overrun by other wave riders. For that reason we've not included such spots in this publication. If you're a good enough surfer with a respectful attitude, you'll find them if you look for them, in due course. As the old surfing adage goes, "Seek and ye shall find!"

Swell prediction

how to figure out when the surf's going to pump

If you live by the coast, or have a boss who'll give you time off whenever you want it, then you won't ever have to worry about predicting the surf. For the other 99 percent of us, trying to forecast when the next swell will arrive is an integral part of being a surfer.

Not very long ago, surfers were totally dependent on the BBC's long-range weather forecasts but these days you can find out when there's going to be surf at the click of a mouse. To start with, if you go to surfgirlmag.com you'll find a whole heap of useful pointers that will tell you when and where the surf will arrive. The charts and services have been colour coded to make life easy. But it's still useful to know how surf is formed so we run through it below. Check out the charts when you've learned the basics.

Three factors determine the size and type of surf generated by a low pressure system: the wind speed out at sea where the swell is being formed, the duration the wind blows, and the fetch (the distance of open ocean the wind blows across). Big clean swells are generated by strong winds blowing across long fetches of the ocean, many hundreds of miles away. Gentle breezes that blow short distance will only produce small choppy waves.

As waves travel across large distances of ocean something weird happens and they 'organise' themselves, eventually arriving in perfect lines, with regular sets of bigger waves. These sets usually contain four to six waves. Ocean swells move at 20 to 25 mph, so a swell generated by a low in the mid Atlantic will typically take three or four days to arrive on our shores.

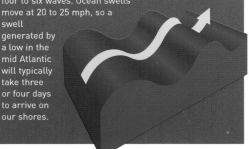

weather charts

Reading the charts may seem difficult at first but with a bit of perserverance you'll soon reap the rewards. By learning about weather charts you can begin to predict when a new swell will hit, how big it'll be, and be ready on the beach when it arrives! The surfgirlmag.com website contains many charts that will show you the weather patterns so that you can track the swell in easy colour coded graphs, and it also gives you up to date surf checks as well as many real time surf webcams.

So no more disappointing trips to the beach to find out the surf's flat. Hurray!

WEDNESDAY

So, you've clicked onto the site and you have weather a chart in front of you...what the hell does it all mean?
The isobars are the lines on a weather map. They actually represent 'contours' of atmospheric pressure. The important thing to know about isobars is that winds blow roughly parallel to them. So the closer the isobars, the stronger the wind.
• **Low pressure systems** (depressions) are the swirling storm systems that generate most swells as they track across the ocean. The strong winds associated with lows rotate in an anti-clockwise direction.
• **High pressure systems** ('anti-cyclones') bring dry sunny weather and light winds, so they usually don't generate much swell. Winds rotate around highs in a clockwise direction.

JAE {WHITE+BLUE}

WOMENS SURF

SPRING 2004
WOMENS SURF

etnies
QUALITY
FOOTWEAR
SINCE 1986

SURF GIRLS
B.E.A.R®

www.beareurope.com

Types of chart

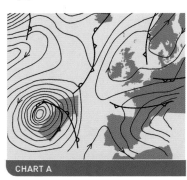

CHART A

CHART A shows a deep low pressure system in the mid Atlantic. The blue arrow shows the area where swell is being generated, and the direction it's travelling in. This low will produce a big southwest swell, heading straight for Devon, Cornwall, Wales and southwest Ireland. It should also provide waves for the Channel Islands and the South Coast. If the area of high pressure centred over Britain stays put for a few days, the result will be offshore winds in most areas giving classic surfing conditions. Cool!

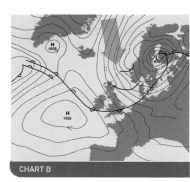

CHART B

CHART B shows an ideal weather map for Scotland and the East Coast, with a low centred over Scandinavia. The strong northerly airflow coming down from the Arctic will generate a powerful north swell, which will arrive a couple of days later; by that time the next low will be approaching from the west, bringing southwest winds—bang offshore!

Swell charts like this colour code information from weather charts to show us the size of the waves, and the arrows show the direction in which they will travel. You can see storms and the waves they are creating travelling across oceans.

Waves bouy readings are commonly available on the internet. They measure the size of the waves passing underneath them and the wind strength and direction. On this particular day the buoy off Cornwall showed a two metre swell with southeasterly winds which was producing perfect surf in the southwest.

gravis

Checking the surf

what to look out for

OK, so you've just arrive at the beach and you're gagging for it. It would be easy to throw off all your clothes with gay abandon and rush into the water. Granted, this impulse is hard to resist, but more often than not you have to go through the rituals of the surf check.

Surf checking is an art and can make or break a decent surf. Those other chaps staring wistfully into the sun aren't just doing the mean and moody look just for your benefit. Well maybe they are, but there are several things you should be looking at.

First things first, before you leave home you should know what the wind and surf is doing from the surf check forecasts. You should know whether the swell is picking up or dropping off and which way the wind's blowing. You should also know what the tide is doing and have some knowledge of the best states of tides and conditions the beaches in your area. (Check out the guides on page 94 for a lowdown of the main surfing breaks.)

MAKE SURE YOU CHECK OUT THE BEACH SET UP BEFORE HEADING INTO THE SURF.

Alex Williams

Once you arrive at the beach, check the beach setup not only for the best place to surf, but also for hazards. If in doubt about hazards or conditions never be afraid to ask the locals. Most would rather you asked than see you plunge headlong into danger and get into trouble.

It goes without saying that if you're a beginner you should stay within the black-and-white chequered flags zone for now, so that the lifeguards can keep an eye on you if you get into trouble. Once you've become more experienced and you feel that you want to move out of the chequered zone, you need to suss out where the best place to surf is. These are the main things you should look out for:

crowds

Note where the main packs of surfers are. The most crowded area is probably where the best waves are, but not always. You should also remember that if all the surfers are all over in one corner fighting it out, they may be leaving open another area. It may not be quite as big, but it could provide you with more rides than having to hassle everyone else.

hazards

Always be aware of any hazards, like rocks and rip currents, and any obstacles that may come into play if the tide is dropping back or pushing in. Note where the rips are. If you are experienced and know how to use them properly they may be able to help you get out the back. If not, they are your biggest hazard so keep away from them.

currents

The other thing to notice is if there is any current. Current usually runs across a beach from right to left or vice versa, and can also be called drift. The direction of a current will determine your entry point into the water. Currents can be just as hazardous as rips, sweeping you along the coast and toward rocks.

sandbanks

As the tide moves, it will cover different sandbanks that may provide richer pickings than the crowded areas. Make sure you know your sandbanks and breaks. There's nothing more disappointing than rushing in somewhere only for it to go flat or the tide get too high.

the sets

Time the sets, they should come in consistently on a time frame called a wave period. It's usually between 10 to 20 minutes. If you know how often the sets are coming in, you can time your paddle so you get out in between them. Otherwise you will spend hours battling against them and wear yourself out. Also, if you know when the sets are coming, you can paddle out and get into position before anyone else knows what's going on. Sneaky hey?

Most spots will have optimum conditions and a wave height ceiling. If it's too big at one spot then others may be just right. Wait and watch two sets come through so you can accurately gauge how big it actually is before deciding where to go in.

ESTPIX

flags on the beach

Always observe warning flags and restricted-area flags. These are used for safety purposes by lifeguards at most of the main surfing beaches from May to September.

If a **red flag** is flying, the beach is closed because surf conditions are unsafe. Beginner and intermediate surfers should find a more sheltered beach elsewhere. Experienced surfers who paddle out when a red flag is flying do so at their own risk.

A zone with **black-and-white chequered flags** is a lifeguard-supervised area for beginner surfers. These areas sometimes get pretty crowded, with boards flying around all over the place, so keep your wits about you.

A zone with **yellow-and-red flags** is an area for swimmers (and bodyboarders) only.

what and what not to do

Once you're ready to charge into the surf, here are a few ground rules to abide by. Remember that most accidents are caused by inexperienced people. It's your duty to learn and adhere to the rules for the sake of your safety and that of others.

Don't throw your board. If a big wave comes through don't panic and throw your board away without checking it isn't going to hit someone. It's never a good idea to rely on your leash anyway, but if you just let go of your board in crowded surf, then the chances are you're going to hurt someone. A loose board with the power of wave behind it is like a weapon. It's the most likely way to hurt someone. Your board is your responsibility. Keep a hold of it.

Don't let your ego write cheques your body can't pay. Surfing is about pushing your limits, but don't be stupid. The ocean will always weed out the weaklings so always be aware of your own abilities and limits.

Don't panic. There probably isn't a situation that you can get yourself in that someone else hasn't already been in and dealt with. If you get out of your depth, calmly ask for help or assess the situation and deal with it logically. The hazards section will explain how to prepare for and deal with emergencies.

Don't surf alone. It's safer to surf with a mate or two...and a lot more fun.

Don't surf straight after a meal, or after drinking alcohol.

Do observe warning flags and restricted-area flags (see box). These are used for safety purposes by lifeguards at most of the main surfing beaches from May to September.

Do check your equipment. Make sure your board has no unrepaired dings that could cut you, check that your leash is free of nicks or kinks. Wax the deck of your board so that it's nice and grippy all over.

Chris Power

Rules of the waves

One thing that you've got to be aware of before you enter the surf is etiquette. Like a medieval joust, the rules of surfing go back into the mists of times and are a basic highway code of the ocean. It is vitally important that you know and adhere to these rules. They not only self-regulate the sharing of waves, but also makes sure everyone stays safe.

● **The drop-in rule.** If someone is riding then it is their wave and you shouldn't get in their way or try and ride the same wave. This is for two reasons: (A) it would ruin their ride and (B) if you try and takeoff on a wave that a surfer is already speeding along it can lead to painful collisions.

dominique munroe has priority

don't do this... *paddle away into the whitewater and let the surfer on the wave go first*

The basic rule is the person nearest to the peak, (or breaking part of the wave) has priority. If someone is already riding do not paddle for or attempt to catch it. If you do this, it is called "dropping in" or "burning" and is one of surfings cardinal sins.

● **The oncoming surfer has priority.** If someone is riding a wave and you are paddling out, do not try to paddle in front of them. Paddle into the whitewater and let them go past. This is one of the most commonly broken rules. It's really frustrating for the rider to see someone ignoring their existence rather than using common sense and paddling out of the way. And it's dangerous. The safest way to deal with oncoming surfers is to put yourself where they definitely don't want to be, in the whitewater. If in doubt, stop paddling and sit up where you are. This makes sure there is no confusion and the surfer can take the appropriate action.

● **All lineups have locals**, regulars who pretty much dominate the lineup. Basically this means the best, fittest or longest serving members of the pack will get the most waves. The hierarchy will usually go something like this; the older surfers who have been at a break a long time, the local hotties, then the visiting hotties, and down through the ability levels to the learners. When you paddle out, try and check out how the lineup is working and how you fit in it.

Most of the time you're in the water you're basically waiting your turn. If you do this, your turn will come. Trouble only usually happens when people jump in at a spot and ignore what's actually happening, basically queue jumping. If this happens, the queuing system breaks down making it worse for everyone. If surfers see you are waiting then more often than not they'll let you join the system. Once you've been accepted into the system by the locals you'll almost be guaranteed waves.

dropping in *priority – going right* *going left* *pull back!*

paddle out of the way

Tara Moller

Estpix

Voodoo Dolls

WWW.VOODOODOLLS.COM
UK INFO PHONE: +44 (0) 1626 362883 FAX: +44 (0) 1626 354599
E-MAIL: ENQUIRIES@VOODOODOLLS.COM

Hazards

surfboards

For beginners, the biggest hazards to watch out for are surfboards—other people's and your own. Whenever you lose control, try to jump off the back of your board and land behind it. As you come back up to the surface, cover you're head with your arms. If you see someone else's board hurtling towards you, the best course of action is to duck under the water. Surfboards are highly buoyant objects so if you duck two or three feet underwater you'll be safe. Again, cover your head with your arms as you come up to the surface.

ROCHELLE BALLARD DEMONSTRATES THE OCCUPATIONAL HAZARDS OF BEING ONE OF THE WORLDS MOST FEARLESS WOMEN SURFERS.

rip currents

Water pushed towards a beach by the action of waves flows back out to sea as a rip current. Rips can usually be identified from the shore as channels of deeper water (often between sandbars) where the waves aren't breaking; the surface of the water is usually rippled or choppy, and may be discoloured by suspended sand. A strong rip current can quickly drag an inexperienced surfer out to sea. If you get caught in a rip, don't try to paddle back to shore against the current; instead, paddle across it to wherever the waves are breaking. Rip currents are often only 10 or 20 yards wide, so you can usually escape their clutches by paddling a short distance. Never leave your board, it's your life raft.

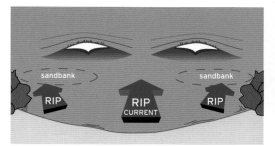

rocks

If you're surfing a rocky reef or pointbreak, wear boots (and a maybe a helmet if it's a really gnarly spot). When you wipeout, try to land feet-first; never dive off forwards at a shallow break.

RIDERS
UNLIMITED

www.oxboweb.com

OXBOW

Emergencies

Accidents happen, it's a fact of life. Whether they're caused by foolishness or plain bad luck, it makes no difference. At the end of the day, the guys who handle tough situations are the guys who know what to do in an emergency. The following is only intended as a basic guide to emergency action. Every surfer should do a course in water safety, rescue skills and resuscitation. The question you should ask yourself is this: if your best mate was in serious trouble, would you know what to do to help?

water rescue procedure

If you're on the beach or in the water and you see or hear someone in distress, you may need to perform a water rescue. Here's what to do:
1. Assess the situation. Do NOT risk your own life if you are not sufficiently experienced in the prevailing conditions. Be especially wary of rip currents, rocks and caves. Establish what needs to be done, and what assistance is needed.
2. Send for help. Alert the lifeguards at the nearest lifeguard station, or phone the coastguard (dial 999). Get assistance from other surfers, especially locals who are likely to be more confident in rough conditions.
3. If you are absolutely confident that you can assist the person in trouble without putting your own life at risk, then act quickly by going to their aid. Always use a rescue aid, such as your surfboard or a Peterson tube.
4. The person in trouble may well be distressed or in shock. Talk to him as you approach; try to sound confident, even if you are nervous. When you're about six feet away, pass your board (or rescue aid) to him. Do not allow him to grab you.
5. Keep the person calm and reassured. If you know help is on its way, it may be best to wait for assistance.
6. If no help is coming, or the situation requires immediate action, place the person on your board and paddle into shore, lying on top of him. Be aware of approaching waves, and keep the patient secure on the board. An unconscious casualty must be brought back to shore as quickly as possible; if he is not breathing, start mouth-to-nose respiration (see below).
7. Once back on the beach give the appropriate aftercare.

the ABC of resuscitation

A – Airway
Open the airway by lying the person flat on his back, lifting his jaw and tilting the head back. Carefully remove any obstructions from the mouth.

B – Breathing
Check the person is breathing. Look to see if his chest is rising and falling; listen and feel for his breath against your cheek.

C – Circulation
Check the pulse. Find the pulse by placing your fingers against the side of the Adam's apple (voice box) and pressing gently down.
• If there is a pulse and the casualty is breathing, put him in the recovery position (lying on his side with the head tilted back to keep the airway open).
• If there is a pulse but no breathing, start mouth-to-mouth (or mouth-to-nose if at sea) respiration:
   a. Pinch the casualty's nostrils firmly shut and open the airway.
   b. Take a deep breath and seal your lips around the casualty's lips. Blow into the mouth watching the chest rise. Let the chest fall completely. Continue at about 10 breaths per minute, checking the pulse after every 10 breaths.
   c. Once the casualty starts breathing, put him in the recovery position.
• If there is no pulse and no breathing, start mouth-to-mouth respiration and chest compression:
   a. Give two breaths of mouth-to-mouth.
   b. Place the heel of your hand two fingers' breadth above the junction of the rib margin and the sternum (breastbone). Place your other hand on top and interlock your hands.
   c. Keeping your arms straight, press down by no more than two inches. Then relax the pressure to allow the heart to refill. Continue compressions at a rate of 80 per minute, but pause every 15 compressions to give two breaths of mouth-to-mouth.
   d. Keep checking the pulse. Stop chest compression as soon as a pulse returns.
NEVER start chest compression if the heart is beating.
DO NOT GIVE UP until medical assistance arrives.

bleeding

If the victim has a bad cut, raise the part of the body which is bleeding (if possible), and use a clean pad to apply direct external pressure to the site of the wound. Seek medical help immediately.

hypothermia

Immersion in cold water can lead to hypothermia if the body temperature drops below 95°F. Both the nervous system and muscles are affected so symptoms may include shivvering, slurred speech, and difficulty in thinking clearly. If the condition becomes severe, death can result through heart failure so immediate action is necessary. Protect the victim from the cold. Get assistance from the lifeguards and call an ambulance. Remove the victim's wet clothing or wetsuit, and warm up his body by covering him with dry blankets or clothes. Other ways to raise the body temperature are to place the victim in a lukewarm, body-temperature (not hot!) bath; or to share your own body heat by getting into a sleeping bag together.

useful websites

To find a St Johns Ambulance lifesaver or first aid course near you got to
www.sja.org.uk/training

For details on the SLSC lifeguard training courses email: training@lifeguards.org.uk
http://www.lifeguards.org.uk

BOARD ANGELS
THE WINGS OF HAPPINESS
Kangaroo Poo
since 1985

Why surf schools are cool

Everyone feels differently about their first surfing experience. For some it is love at first wave, for others it can be a hard fought battle against the elements that can put them off for life. With the first experience being so crucial to a life-long love affair with surfing, it's a good idea to make that first time as easy and enjoyable as it can be. Here top British surfer **Sarah Bentley** explains why it's a good idea to start off at a surf school.

Learning with a British Surfing Association approved surf school is a great way of lessening the trauma of taking to the waves for the first time. A surf school will supply all the necessary equipment and will provide a fun and safe situation in which to learn. All instructors need to hold both a BSA teaching certificate, which means that the tuition you receive will follow a proven structure, and a NARS Lifeguard Qualification so you will be well looked after. Choosing to go with a surf school also means that you will be sharing the experience with a group of people in the same position, adding to the fun factor and creating that important bit of friendly competitiveness.

My advice for approaching surfing lessons would be to begin with a two-hour starter lesson. This will give you the very basics and will help you to work out whether or not it is for you. It is important not to get too dismayed if you don't manage to stand up on your first lesson. It can take a long time to get to the point, where you start to feel at one with the ocean and your surfing equipment. As surfing possesses one of the steepest learning curves of any sport, and involves so many different elements, it can take time and a level of commitment to start enjoying yourself. It is also dependent on environmental conditions which make it one of the most frustrating, but at the same time, enjoyable things to do.

If you feel that you want to progress a little further it is well worth signing up for a few more sessions before heading out on your own and splashing out on your own board, wetsuit and accessories. In doing this you can get the most from your surf instructor as they can assist you with any specific difficulties that you might have. Don't be scared to ask them questions about any aspect of the sport, as surfers are always keen to give advice especially if they get a chance to recount in graphic detail their own experiences!

There are several girls' surf schools in the UK and they offer a range of different packages including morning or afternoon lessons, full-day tuition or weekend specials. Surfboards and wetsuits are provided, so all you have to bring is a towel, swimming costume and your enthusiasm. As females learn differently from men the teaching is more tailored to women's needs. There is less chance of feeling inhibited and intimidated as when learning in a mixed group. As with all BSA approved surf schools, a session will start with an explanation of the equipment, safety advice and a run through of the basic techniques before heading out into the water.

Being taught the correct techniques by a properly-qualified instructor will save you hours of frustration. Lessons are inexpensive and good fun. Most importantly, it's vital that you learn about safety in the water: the ocean is a dangerous place if you don't know what you're doing.

Girls' surf schools in the UK

Hibiscus. The UK's first women-only surf school, based in Newquay. Go to www.hibiscussurfschool.co.uk for more info.
Let's Go Surf Tracy Boxall has opened up a surf school in South Wales. Go to www.letsgosurf.co.uk for more info.
Walking On Waves Sarah Whitely's surf school, based in North Devon. Go to www.walkingonwaves.co.uk for more info.
St Agnes Surf Academy Dominique Munroe and Sarah Bentley set this up with an emphasis on coaching local budding surf girls and adding more longevity to the idea of just coaching the basics. For more info call Dominique on 01209 890337.
SurfGirl courses Run in conjunction with the English Surf Federation, SurfGirl magazine operates lessons, weekend courses and holidays for beginners through to advanced riders. Go to surfgirlmag.com for more details or the ESF website www.englishsurfschool.com
Bodyboarding To gain confidence in the waves, many girls try bodyboarding. Check out www.robbarber.com for expert tuition.
For a list of BSA approved surf schools go to www.britsurf.co.uk

Essentials

Buying the right equipment you need to be a successful surfer is essential. Your board and wetsuit are your tickets to ride, so don't make the wrong choice. It's your money, time and sanity that's at stake! To give you a clear idea of what you need before you go into the surf shop here's SurfGirl's lowdown.

the marvels of modern industry and
science make it possible for us to have
more choices now than ever before
relatively unimportant decisions can expand
to fill hours and hours if we do not
limit ourselves to a reasonable number of
options

Barry Schwartz, 'The Paradox of Choice'

Surfboards

It's vitally important to pick the right board for your size, shape and ability. This will allow your surfing to develop. Here we take a look at surfboards and top tips for buying the right board for you.

There are three main types of surfboard, soft boards, moulded boards, and custom boards, all available in a range of sizes and shapes.

Soft surfboards (or foamies) are made from a semi-rigid plastic foam which is soft and very buoyant. They're ideal for first-time surfers, and are consequently widely used by surf schools.

Moulded surfboards Once you've mastered the basics on a soft board you should move on to a more rigid board which will have much more drive. A moulded board is constructed by joining two moulded-fibreglass halves of the board together, then filling the middle with liquid polyurethane foam which then hardens. Modern moulded boards (brands like NSP, Resin8 and SurfTech) are harder wearing than custom boards, so they're ideal for novice surfers who've done a few days' tuition at a surf school and want to move on.

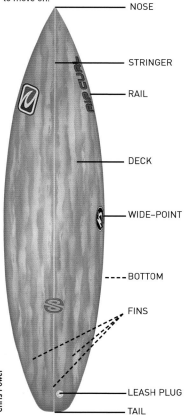

- NOSE
- STRINGER
- RAIL
- DECK
- WIDE-POINT
- BOTTOM
- FINS
- LEASH PLUG
- TAIL

Chris Power

Cazanave

FRENCH PRO MARIE-PIERRE ABRIGAL WITH HER QUIVER OF BOARDS.

Custom surfboards are made by hand from polyurethane foam blanks which are shaped and then covered with a thin layer of fibreglass. These boards can be made to any shape or design required, with any colour scheme. They're lightweight, but easily damaged. Suitable for beginners and experts alike, custom boards cost £250-£350. If you're buying your first board, think volume. A big, high-volume board will be stable, easy to paddle, and catch a lot of waves. Generally, a beginner's board should be at least 12" longer than you are tall, and thick enough to provide plenty of buoyancy. Seek advice about what sort of board you should buy from a friend who surfs, or a reputable surf shop.

Secondhand A secondhand board can be a good bet if it's suitable for you and free of defects; a few dents in the deck are nothing to worry about, but delamination can be a real problem. Dings that have been properly fixed won't affect performance but avoid snapped boards which have been "repaired as good-as-new" according to the salesman, as these are prone to snap again and the rocker may well be out of line. Again, seek advice from a

TRACEY BOXALL SHOWS US HER BOARD.

Progressing

As you progress upwards from your lonely struggles in the white water and onto the green faces you're going to want a new board. The fastest way to learn is by gradually reducing your boards' length as your skill and strength increases. Remember jumping straight onto a shortboard is just like jumping into a formula one car without taking any lessons. Not only will you not be able to handle the speed and manoeuvrability, but you won't be able to paddle it or catch any waves.

The first four boards below may act as a rough guide through this progression. After the initial 'foamy' learning period, progression should be made onto a mini mal or fun board, then a large thruster and finally onto the modern high performance shortboard. Give yourself time to get used to each board before moving onto a shorter model. Board five is a double ender which is an ideal high performance summer board.

Bullet board.
8'0" x 21-1/2 x 3-3/4

Down The Line
Slipper
7'0" x 21-7/8" x 2-3/8"
Shaped by Nigel Semmens.

Beach Beat
Fatboy Flyer
7'2" x 20-1/2" x 2-5/8"
Shaped by Chops Lascelles.

Local Hero
Shortboard
6'8" x 19-1/8" x 2-1/4"
Shaped by Graeme Bunt.

Nigel Semmens
Double Ender
6'2" x 19-1/4" x 2-3/8"
Shaped by Nigel Semmens.

Buying your first board

If you've had a couple of lessons and are certain you've got the bug it's time to buy a board. Surf shops are full of colourful sleek designs but at this stage it's vitally important and that you choose your stick sensibly and allow your surfing to develop. It's no good having a really colourful board if you sink everytime you sit on it!

Chris Power

we asked three top shapers to give us a few pointers

Hawaiian shaper Jeff Bushman comments: "Nine out of ten girls are lighter than guys and generally haven't been surfing as long so wouldn't need something as tuned as a guy's board at the same length. I take into account their level of ability but don't shape anything too big that doesn't manoeuvre easily. For example, a guy's board might be 18-1/8 inches wide, with the equivalent girl's board at 18-1/2 inches."

Swansea shaping guru John Purton advises: "Don't get anything too long. Considering that the average girl's height is 5'2" or 5'3", they need a maximum of about 7'4". Otherwise the board will be too cumbersome and you will get knocked around by waves. You don't really need a mini-mal with a fat nose but more of a funboard or 'fat boy' shape."

Newquay's top shaper Nigel Semmens says: "Talk to a reputable shaper or shop salesman about what level you are at, and be honest about your ability. Do not go too small too soon, surfing is a long learning curve. Do not try to ride boards beyond your ability, remember surfing is all about having fun so the girl riding the most waves is having the most fun."

tips for buying your first shortboard

Make sure your new shortboard is the right size.
Let's assume the board you learnt to surf on was a secondhand funboard or mini-mal. It's important not to make too big a jump down in size. Sure you want something more responsive and easier to duck-dive, but if you buy a board with insufficient volume you simply won't be able paddle into the waves early enough. In other words don't buy a sexy 6'1" just because it looks cool. (Do you want to be a poser, or do you want to ride waves?) If you're an average sized girl go for something around 6'6" to 6'8" long, by 19" wide, by 2-3/8" thick. When you're ready to move onto a super-short high performance board you'll know it.

Avoid extreme design features.
Simple, clean shapes work in a greater range of conditions than boards with extreme design features such as channels, concaves, wings and so on.

Talk to the shop salesman (or shaper) about your needs.
Any salesman worth his salt really does want to help you choose a board that'll suit your ability so ask his opinion. If you like the look of a board, make sure that the brand is an established one; you'll get a well-built board from a reputable company. Don't be afraid to get recommendations from different shops before buying a board.

Make any necessary safety modifications.
If the board doesn't have a noseguard, buy one and stick it on. If the trailing edges of the fins are sharp, blunt them off with sandpaper.

Go surf ya brains out.
At first you'll probably feel pretty wobbly on your new board, since it'll be a lot less stable than your old plank. But what you lose in stability, you gain in manoeuvrability. Once you get your feet in the right place and find the 'sweet spot', you'll know you've made the right move. Work at your new relationship – it'll take

Mike Searle

5'11 x 19 3/4" x 2 3/8" TWIN 3592

Surfboards: what's really goin' on?

Getting to know a bit about how your surfboard works can help your surfing no end. But board design is a complex thing. So what are the most important design features of a surfboard? We asked a couple of Britain's top shapers to give us the low-down.

volume

"Volume is really important," says Pete 'Chops' Lascelles of Beach Beat Surfboards. "If I'm doing a custom board for someone I always ask their weight so I can decide how much volume to use for that person. It's important that a shaper finds out as much as he can about how the girl surfs and the kind of waves she is going to be surfing. When you know those things you get an idea about how much volume to use and you can combine that with the rest of the design features."

rails

"The shape of the rails can go from blocky, to low and soft," explains Nigel Semmens. "The choice is again down to a surfer's preference. A blocky rail sits higher in the water and allows more volume and therefore buoyancy; but if a girl isn't big enough to sink that rail, it'll cause problems. Low-volume rails are easier to bury deep on turns but they're very sensitive and tend to 'catch' or bog down quite a lot unless you're an experienced surfer or you're surfing really perfect waves."

rocker and bottom contours

"The rocker [or bottom curve] is the most important design feature of a board," says Nigel. "It determines how the board turns, the speed of the board, and the planing ability of the board—which are the basic performance fundamentals. The nose of the board can either be flipped quite sharply, or you can have a long soft entry to make the board plane nicely. The tail rocker will determine how the board rides. If you have a lot of tail rocker the board will be very responsive and easy to turn, but it won't plane as easily. If you have a flatter tail, the board will project really fast but it won't turn as easily. So it's up to the shaper to create a happy medium that will suit the rider. There are several other variations of contour a shaper can use on the bottom including concaves, channels, vee and reverse vee, but worrying about these combinations is best left to advanced surfers.

nose rocker

tail rocker

tail shape

swallow tail

squash tail

pin tail

"Rounded square-tails [also called squash tails] are probably the most commonly used tail shape in the world today," says Chops Lascelles. "There are also swallow-tails, pin-tails and rounded pins, but beginners should stick to rounded squares."

planshape

The plan shape is the outline of the board, as seen from above. Planshapes vary considerably from one type of board to another. "If you compare a gun and a shortboard, the two planshapes are as far away from each other as you can get," says Jools from Gulf Stream Surfboards in North Devon. "Most shortboards will have a wider tail, and a bigger planing surface. If you look at the planshape of a big-wave board it will be wider in the nose and narrower in the tail; so the board is better for paddling into big waves, while the tighter tail template allows control in sketchy situations. "If a customer wants a standard 6'8" rounded pin for all-round conditions you'd probably keep the wide point in the middle."

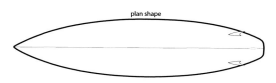

plan shape

More about boards

How to make your relationship last

time to adjust to the new pace of life!

In the early days you will be in love with your new stick. The days will be long and tiring, yet satisfying and fulfilling. However, as with any relationship, if this is going to be a long-term thing it is important that you look after it.

Use protection. All those little dents and bruises from everyday use soon mount up. One day your board will be your dream, the next you'll wake up and it'll seem like it's been beaten with the ugly stick. It's not your board's fault, it's just the wearing effect of the hard knocks of life. So buy your board a decent bag. No one loves worn out old sticks so it could also be difficult to get rid of, and end up hanging around making you feel bad. Look after your stick and you can make a clean break when the time comes.

Keep your board healthy. Saggy and dishevilled just ain't sexy in any language, so keep your partner in tip top condition and you'll be happy with them longer. If you don't mend all your dings quickly all the cracks and dents will suck up water. These will then turn yellow, delaminate and the board will fall apart before your very eyes.

Don't be afraid to pick up other sticks. This is 2004 so it's okay to experiment. Try out some of your friends' models and compare notes. They may look all new, young and sparkley, but all that glitters is not gold and you may find that you don't get on with them as well as you thought. When you return to your old stick you may find comfort in the reliable old beast. If not, well, life is short so ditch the old fella and move on.

Book your board in for a makeover. You'd be surprised how much difference it makes. Remove all the old wax, clean up the bottom and rails, give it a bit of polish and that grubby tatty piece of fibreglass may once again reveal the alluring charms that first excited you. If in the process of makeover you find something serious, or if it still doesn't float your boat, then remember, sometimes you've got to be cruel to be kind.

Variety is the spice of life. Life is a journey and you may need to test out many vehicles on the road to happiness. You may well grow out of your old stick and want to move on. Don't feel all bad or get stuck in a rut as niether of you will end up happy. Be strong, draw the line and move forward. Just remember the favourite things about your last partner and try to build on them with the next.

How boards are made

Nigel Semmens takes us through the board manufacturing process.

1. Making a surfboard is a complex process. First the shaper takes a polyurethane foam blank, decides what kind of board he is going to make and cuts out the outline. Using an expert eye and a steady hand, he then shapes the rocker and the rails and foils out any rough edges.

2. Next the board has a design (which can be customised) sprayed directly onto the foam.

3. Once dry, the board is taken into the glassing bay where layers of fibreglass are applied to the top and bottom with resin.

4. After the glassing process the board has all the rough edges sanded down and one more 'finishing' coat of resin is applied to seal the board's outer casing. Then it's back to the sanding bay to be finely sanded and polished before being delivered to it's eager new owner.

GIRLS DO IT BETTER

Makeovers made easy

Treating your board to a makeover will not only make it look a lot nicer, but also help retain it's value. Ester Spears a few ways you can keep your board looking tip top.

removing the wax from the deck

To do this, leave the board in the sun for ten minutes to soften up the old wax, then scrape it off with the sharp edge of a wax comb or a similar plastic tool. However, really old wax sets like concrete and as we all know the sun doesn't shine in the UK from November until April, so go for the hairdryer option. Apply the heat and softened up a bit the wax will slide off in no time. (If you're doing this at home, do it in the garage or outside – you really don't want to tread a load of manky wax into you're mum's best Persian rug.)

Once old dirty wax is removed, your board will feel lighter and look way better. The last smears of wax can be taken off with a bit of white spirit.

dings – DIY made easy

Small dings can be covered with duct tape for a short term fix but these need sorting out as soon as they are dry. With the products available these days you can mend most breakages in minutes. Here's how.

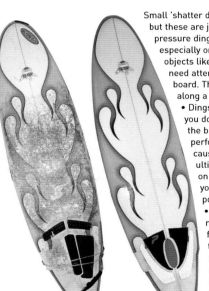

Small 'shatter dings' or 'spider cracks' are common on used boards but these are just cosmetic and don't need to be fixed. Likewise pressure dings – the shallow dents you see on all used boards, especially on the deck; these are caused by impacts from hard objects like your knees (or head!). Minor cracks and dings only need attention if you suspect that they are leaking water into the board. The tell-tale signs of leakage are salt crystals developing along a crack, or yellowing of the foam underneath.

• Dings that penetrate the fibreglass, however, are something you don't want to ignore. Water will seep in, adding weight to the board and possibly affecting its hydrodynamic performance as well. Long-term exposure to water can cause the foam to weaken and collapse, which can ultimately result in a buckled or broken board. Bad cracks on the rails often develop sharp edges that can cut you (or your wetsuit), so these should also be fixed as soon as possible.

• Large holes need to fixed by an expert but small repairs can be done with 'repair putty', applied straight from a tube. There are several products of this type on the market such as Solarez and Sun Cure. They contain resin, particles of fibreglass and hardener all in one, and are activated by UV light. There is no mixing to be done or ratios to get right – the resin simply goes hard when exposed to sunlight. Magic!

• As with every repair job, a little bit of preparation makes the whole job easier. The most important thing is to make sure the ding is dry. If it isn't, then a couple of days drying out in a warm room is needed.

• Next, get any loose particles and dirt out of the repair area. To allow a good bond between the resin and surfboard, the area around the ding should be rough sanded with coarse sandpaper.

• Once the area is prepared, mask it off with tape to stop overspill of the putty and make the job neater. Because the resin starts to harden as soon as it's exposed to sunlight, you need to work with the putty in the shade. Apply small amounts at a time, working out any air bubbles with a lollipop stick and forming the putty to the shape of the board. For rail dings and flat surfaces you can use Sellotape or a sheet of clear plastic on top of the putty to create a finish that will need little or no sanding.

• Once happy with the repair, expose to sunlight.

• After 10 to 30 minutes (depending on the weather), the repair should be okay to sand down. Once hardened, repair putty is bloody hard stuff, so you'll be stoked if you did a tidy job in stage 4. (If you glooped it on all over the place you'll be sanding for hours!)

• Broken tips of tails or noses can be fixed in a similar fashion after first making little moulds using masking tape. Once hardened, sand back to the original shape.

Further reading: The Ding Repair Scriptures, £7.00 (available from orcasurf.co.uk).

Sarra Robertson - Mentawai Islands

Wetsuits

Alex Williams

A good wetsuit is a must for surfing in British waves. Wetsuits are made of neoprene rubber, and there are all sorts of designs and thicknesses to suit different water temperatures. A good all-round choice would be a full-suit (long arms and legs) with 3mm leg and torso panels, and 2mm arms. Make sure the wetsuit fits snugly: there should be no baggy areas, and the legs and arms should be the right length. Unless you have an unusual body shape, you should be able to buy a suitable wetsuit off-the-peg. Custom-made wetsuits are also available. Wetsuits cost around £100-£250.

For added comfort, wear a lycra rash-vest under your wetsuit. This will prevent chaffing under the arms and around the neck. Most British surfers wear neoprene boots, gloves, and hoods during the winter months. When you're shopping for a new wettie you'll come across lots of different features and a fair bit of jargon. Here's a run-down of the most important things to look for.

glued and blindstitched seams
The seams on a winter suit have to be watertight. (If they're not, your suit will be flushed with icy cold water every time you duck-dive a wave. Highly unpleasant!) To achieve this, wetsuit manufacturers glue and blindstitch their seams and add fabric tape to the inside of the seams to strengthen the join.

types of neoprene
Double-lined neoprene
The most commonly used wetsuit material. The neoprene rubber is sandwiched between two layers of nylon fabric that make it tough and resistant to wear and tear.
Single-lined neoprene
Neoprene with one surface of soft smooth rubber. Not as durable as double-lined or mesh neoprene (see below). Often used around the neck and cuffs, where it's comfortable against the skin and provides a good seal. The smoothness of the rubber prevents wetsuit rash (chaffing).

Mesh neoprene
A type of single-lined neoprene with a textured outer surface which makes it more durable. Often used on the torso and arms of winter suits as it reduces the effects of windchill, keeping you warmer.
Super-stretch / Hyper-stretch / Mega-stretch / Xpandx neoprene
Different names given to different types of extra stretchy neoprene built into the shoulder areas of wetsuits for ease of paddling.

types of lining
Titanium-lined neoprene
Titanium has heat-reflecting properties. When a thin layer of titanium particles is laminated onto the neoprene it reflects some of your body heat and increases the efficiency of the wetsuit.
Polypropylene-lined neoprene
Add a thin layer of polypropylene fabric to the inner side of the neoprene (usually on the torso panels) and the end result is improved insulation and heat retention.

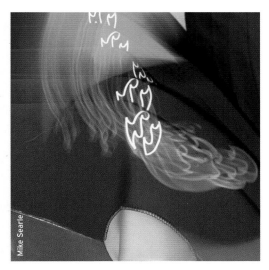

Mike Searle

zip or no zip?
The largest opening in the wetsuit is the one you use to get into it. This presents all sorts of interesting challenges for the wetsuit manufacturer, in particular how to make the suit easy to get on and off, how to seal it so no water gets in, and how to provide maximum flexibility. Various designs are available including zipperless entry systems, conventional zips and short / mini zips. All have pro's and con's; you pay your money and make your choice.

Mike Searle

fit
At the end of the day, the fit of the wetsuit is the most important consideration. If it doesn't fit your body shape correctly all the hi-tech features above will be rendered useless. Every manufacturer uses a slightly different method of tailoring, so you should always try on a few different brands of wetsuit, and then a couple of different sizes of your preferred choice, before you buy.

How to pick the right suit

vest
Ideal temp: 70° (20°C) and above
There are a variety of vests. Basically they offer minimum protection and just keep the windchill off. Some may even claim to reflect body heat back in. They also offer protection from the sun, reefs in the tropics, and stop wax from clogging up in chest hair...although if you're a lady you really should be losing that.

springy
Ideal temp: 66-70° (16-20°C)
Short-arm, short-leg suits are ideal for those days when it's a little too cold for shorts. They are so flexible these days it barely feels like you're wearing one.

long-arm spring and short-arm full suits
Ideal temp: 64-77° (15-22°)
Great flexible suits which are ideal for early summer through to autumn. Short-legs are for surfing in warmer temperature waters, and short-arms for warmer air temps. Strictly speaking, the short arm wettie is better for early summer in the UK.

The 3/2 full suit is the mainstay of the surfer's armoury. In the Southwest you can usually get into them sometime in May if you whack some boots on, and it should keep you warm right up to early winter. (East coast readers forget this bit. You'll still need a 5/3 until mid July!)

If you are going to surf through winter you'll need a 4/3 minimum, but more likely a 5/4/3mm. They are truly amazing these days and will keep you warm for hours on the coldest of days.

don't
1. Never ever wear your rash vest or T shirt over your wetsuit unless you're competing. It serves no purpose and you'll just look silly. If you wear shorts over your wetty you'll look really really silly.
2. Never lend your wetsuit to mates. Especially if they are fat knackers and may stretch it beyond recognition. Doubley so if they're going to pee in it which, let's face it, they all do!
3. Don't hang your wetsuit in the sun. It'll the ruin the rubber and lessen the wetsuits' life.
4. Don't wear your wetsuit back to front.
5. Don't buy a wetty just 'cos it looks nice. Fit is the most important thing. No one looks good in the final throes of hypothermia.
6. Don't force your heels through the calves of the suit trying to get your feet in as you roll around the car park wrestling with your suit. Take care of it!

do
1. Wash out your wetsuit after every surf. Salt perishes the neoprene so rinsing will make it last heaps longer.
2. Use a plastic bag as a sock when putting on a wet wetty. It'll help your feet glide through the legs and prevent damage.
3. Hang your wetsuit on a plastic coat hanger. It'll help it keep it's shape while it dries. If you take it down the beach you can also hang it off the car boot catch and allow the wind to dry it. Cool, eh!
4. Get one of those nifty changing mats that turn themselves into a bag. They'll keep the sand off your suit and protect it while you get changed and keep the stale drainage out of your car boot.
5. Make sure you have the right suit for the conditions you will be surfing in.

Wetsuit accessories

gloves
During the winter, most surfers around the UK will require gloves. There are a wide variety, but again the most important factor is fit.

hoods and hats
An enormous amount of heat is lost through the head. This is especially so when you are constantly diving under waves in the winter. Add in the winter windchill factor and you can see why they are a cosy accessory to own. They also prevent the ears from getting cold and an ailment called 'surfers ear".

wetsuit boots
Wetsuit boots keep you warm in the winter, and offer protection from barnacles and rocks when entering the surf. Depending on the durability and warmth required you can choose various thicknesses of boots. You can also choose from split toe or round toe boots.

Neoprene nightmares

ESTPIX

NICOLA BUNT DEMONSTRATES THE ART OF GETTING IN AND OUT OF RUBBER.

Getting in and out of a wetsuit is an artform. Here author and surfer Lauren McCrossan takes a look at the joys of squeezing into rubber in a crowded car park.

Surfing in the 21st century; so fashionable, so popular. Everyone wants to be part of the surfing craze, from the girl next door to the Hollywood A-list celeb. Designers are using surf-inspired fashion in their collections and major companies unrelated to the sport use surfing images in their adverts. The surfing world is all about athleticism, tropical waters, bikinis, boardies, beautiful bodies and glamour. Well, excuse me, but have any of these people stood in a wind-blown car-park trying to:
a) squeeze into a stiff 5mm wetsuit while maintaining some level of decency, or
b) extricate oneself from the same wetsuit when it's waterlogged, twice as heavy, and one's fingers appear to be suffering from rigor mortis?

My first wetsuit was a generous (to use the term lightly) gift from a friend back when I knew little about surfing and especially about how to surf and look moderately cool simultaneously. It was also rare at the time to stumble across off-the-peg wetsuits designed just for girls, i.e. with all the right bits going in and out at all the right places. Despite being neon bubblegum pink, this suit had definitely not been designed with a girl's figure in mind. In fact, how any human being could get in and out of the thing and surf without dislocating several joints was beyond me. The neoprene was so stiff the suit could stand up on its own. I have no doubt it could have surfed on its own too, as it certainly had a mind of its own. I needed manual assistance to put it on. Once it was zipped up in a straitjacket-like fashion, I took care to avoid all shiny surfaces for fear of catching a glimpse of my own reflection. Mind you, I could well imagine how I looked. My body is short and my legs long in comparison. This suit was quite the opposite and also had space for dangly bits that I don't possess to fill it. There was no

nipping in at the waist and my breasts — for which no allowance had been made — were squashed to fried egg proportions. The whole experience was traumatising and, I admit, often culminated in a tearful scene when I tried to remove the damn thing without requiring a surgical procedure or losing my skin in the process.

Thankfully the major surf labels woke up to the plight of us surf girls. "Ooh look," I imagine one of them commenting in the early 90s, "there are girls in the line-up and, what d'ya know, their bodies look different to ours. Shall we make them suits that fit or shall we carry on making them wear uncomfortable suits for men just in case they end up surfing better than us?"

So we got suits of our own with flattering seams, appealing colour schemes and even, in some cases, decorative flowers or angel wings. In truth, though, the variety and quality of the suits for girls, as far as warmth and flexibility are concerned, still fall behind the ranges for men but rapid progress is being made. The initial problem for a girl is finding a cut that fits snugly, given the fact that we tend to be such diverse shapes and sizes (or as I like to say 'unique'). Nevertheless, between the different cuts of all the major brands now available, there is usually one that will be close to the mark.

Which then simply leaves the task of getting the wetsuit on and making it to the sea with a modicum of pride left. Now this may be a generalisation, but I have noticed during my time spent in the aforementioned wind-blown car-parks, that male surfers have no problem with stripping off in public to don their wetsuits. While I struggle to keep an oversized beach towel up around my bare chest and hurriedly shove my underwear out of sight, all around me men are baring white bums and chicken giblet manifestations that I would rather not have to cop an eyeful of. Of course, I could avert my eyes but I'm looking at them to see if they are looking at me when my towel slips and with it my modesty!

Amazingly, wetsuit designers resisted the urge to design for that fantasy world where we all have figures like Elle MacPherson. Naturally, how you look in a wetsuit has no bearing on how well you surf and in a perfect world of high self-esteem, we would all strut confidently down the beach in our skin-tight rubber to merrily dominate the line-up. After all, not every guy who surfs has a body like Kelly Slater to carry off the wetsuit look and they don't seem to mind. In reality, however, I know lots of girls who have reservations about revealing all to the world in something even less flattering than a school PE kit, especially when they are just starting to surf. One friend dreaded meeting anyone she knew on the beach,

ESTPIX

EASKEY BRITTON SHOWS HOW SPARE YOUR BLUSHES!

and another considered learning to surf in the dark (do not try this at home!) There is something courageous about taking up a sport that requires you to parade along a public beach in a figure-hugging suit while trying not to feel as if you have several refugees stowed about your person, before having to flounder in the whitewater for months (or in my case years) until you can rightly claim to be a surfer.

The thing is, all this considered, the moment I immerse myself in the icy waters of Britain or Ireland, I am so thankful for my thick wetsuit, boots and gloves. Despite my ability to shiver in the ocean in Hawaii, with the right practical equipment I am toasty warm and able to surf for a couple of hours without my heart stopping from hypothermia. More than simple practicality, however, when I paddle for the wave of the day, jump up and ride it all the way to the beach, I don't care what people think of how I look in my wetsuit. In fact, let them look because after the sheer exhilaration of a perfect wave, I feel ready to strut up that beach as if I am Layne Beachley. As for the balancing towel act during the wetsuit removal process, who needs it? I can strip off with pride; liberated by that wave, which may not have looked magical to some but which certainly felt magical to me. So much so, that I know I will be back again tomorrow... and the next day... and the day after that, wetsuit and all.

Accessories

A surfboard, some wax and a wetsuit are the bare essentials that you'll need to go surfing. But on top of that there's a hundred and one accessories that you can buy. We'd recommend the following kit for a comfortable life surfing in our harsh climate.

Leashes

A leash is the piece of equipment that will stop you endlessly swimming back to shore to get your board back after you've wiped out. It is a stretchy urethane cord fixed to the tail of the surfboard and attached to your ankle by a velcro wraparound strap. When choosing a leash look at your boards length and choose a leash targeted to that size, usually, for longer boards there is a choice of knee or ankle fastenings; its worth asking for help when it comes to leashes.

Noseguards

If you've decided to shortboard, depending on the tip of your board your going to want a noseguard. A rubber mould to glue on the tip of your board, the guard will prevent injury during any of those nasty wipeouts. Injuries are pretty rare but when they do occur they tend to be as a result of collision between you and either the nose or fins of your board. Better safe than sorry!

Wax/deck grip

You need to apply a good liberal layer of wax on a new board to give you grip and it's useful to apply a light coating of wax each time you surf. You should apply it mostly where your feet are going to be positioned, but it's good to have a bit all over for added grip especially on rails where you will push up with your hands.

When you have progressed further with your surfing you may choose to use deck grip. This allows you more grip for your back foot during the more technical manoeuvres.

Rash vest

To prevent wetsuit rub, you should go for a compressed neoprene rash vest with titanium lining and Lycra rash protection; you'll also benefit from increased warmth.

Wetsuit bags

There are a wide variety of wetsuit bags, from backpacks with wet and dry pockets to changing mats that transform into bags. The latter are great as they also protect your suit when getting in and out of them. Backpacks are better for travel.

Board bags

Essential to keep your board free from dings. Most damage happens to boards while on land; getting them in and out of the house, the car, and onto planes. A knitted cotton sock will provide protection from the sun, and gentle bumps and scrapes. A padded bag will prevent all sorts of damage during day or short trips. The big travel bags are designed to protect a number of boards during international travel.

Sunglasses

Often thought of as a fashion item, sunglasses are essential to surfers. Eyes that are exposed to the sun's rays bouncing off the sand and sea day after day can lea to damaged corneas, and squinting to wrinkles. Always buy a decent pair of glasses with high grade UV A and B protection.

First Steps

Surfing is not an easy sport to master. As a beginner you face a long and arduous road, yet it's filled with pitstops of euphoria; the first time you get to your feet, the first green wave – they're all milestones to being a surfer.

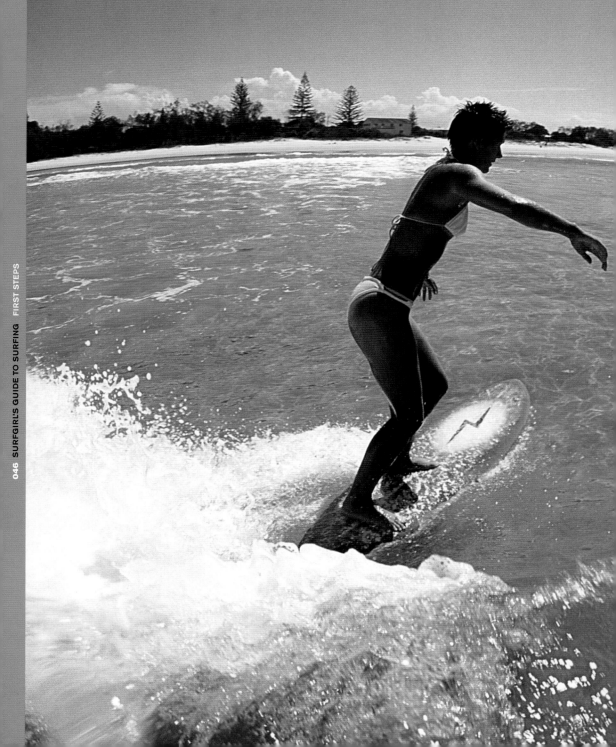

the journey of a thousand miles
must begin with a single step

Lao Tzu, father of Taoism

First steps

So you're ready to take the plunge. You've had a few lessons, you've been and bought the right size board for you (which should be a big, thick, wide board) and now you're ready to learn to surf. Top surf instructor Tracy Boxall takes us through the early learning stages.

TRACEY BOXALL RIPPING IN WESTERN AUSTRALIA.

carrying your board

To begin with it may sound pretty basic but once you've got your own board, you don't want to destroy it by dragging it along the beach. You need to learn how to carry it. There are two ways to do this; the first is to put the fin in towards your body, though I have found that this can be very hard when you don't have the arm length; the second way is to put the fin in front so that you can see it and can avoid hitting anyone with it.

attaching your leash

Now you're at the water's edge ready to go in. Firstly you need to be connected with your surfboard by a leash. See the way I'm putting it on in the photo. Make sure the cord comes away from your leg on the heel side. Don't position the cord coming away from the inside of your ankle otherwise you will be tripping all over the place.

getting to your feet

Before attempting to stand up you, need to determine which foot you are going to have at the front of your board and which at the back. Practice which way feels the most comfortable when you are on the beach and then remember, the foot that is going at the back is the one that you attach your leash too.

Position your hands under your chest and push yourself up into a standing position in one smooth movement. Lead with your front foot and aim to keep central in order to keep the board stable. Your feet should be about a metre apart, and assume a crouched position, with a low centre of gravity for balance. Stand with your back foot at 90 degrees to the board's stringer (central line), and your front foot at 45 degrees. Look where you're going, not at your feet.

alternative way

The second technique that you can use is more of a 'crawl up' rather than a leap to your feet. Many girls may find this technique easier to get to grips with at first until your arm and shoulder muscles become stronger to enable a one movement hop up.

wrong way

You don't want to to this. Make sure that you lie straight on your board otherwise it will upset your balance. And keep your legs together and in the centre of the board, as it creates drag in the water.

walking out

Right it's now time to hit the water. Remember only go out in small surf while you're learning. First of all walk out to waist depth water, making sure your surfboard is pointing straight out to sea. Hold your board to one side. You don't want your surfboard between you and the wave, as the board will hit you.

takeoff

Once you're at waist depth, turn and point your surfboard towards the beach. Make sure it's straight. When the white water is about to hit the tail of your surfboard you need to push up.

Lie on your surfboard in the trim position, which is lying straight on your surfboard with your hands underneath your chest, legs together. Then push up, and lean left or right. Get yourself used to your surfboard by experimenting with your weight distribution. Lean forward and it will speed you up, slide back and it will slow you down. By leaning left or right you can get used to steering. On small days you can learn to ride unbroken waves. So practice paddling out, pushing up over the waves and sitting on your surfboard. Remember to enjoy yourself!

DOMINIQUE MUNROE

PR(O)TEST
ALL CONDITIONS BOARDWEAR
WWW.PROTESTBOARDWEAR.CO

PROTEST

BOARD ANGELS RIDIN IN STYLE
SUMMER 2004
PROTEST / THE ALL CONDITIONS BOARDWEAR COMPANY

Exercise

getting fit and increasing your strength is essential if you want to improve your surfing.

These exercises target a lot of the muscles used in surfing and can help if you are learning to surf and want to get to your feet quicker. I found that when I increased my training to go on tour, everything felt easier, from getting to my feet, to pulling off wicked manoeuvres. Being a small-framed person, having that extra strength helped me so much with my surfing. I was able to put my body into positions I didn't think I could when landing big moves. If, like me, you hate going to the gym because you find it intimidating, or you feel embarrassed, well relax, you're not alone, quite a lot of women feel the same way. Here are some exercises that you can do at home while watching your favourite soap. It should only take about 15 minutes, three times per week. You should try these exercises on alternate nights. There are four exercises and you should build your way up to three sets of between 10 and 15 repetitions of each. If you are able to do only one set of 10 of each exercise that's fine, you can increase the amount weekly.

– Tracy Boxall

press ups

Beginner's option
Begin on your hands and knees with your hands shoulder width apart and your feet slightly raised off the floor. Make sure your back is straight by pulling your belly button up to your spine and clenching your buttocks. Bend your arms until your chin is close to the ground and push yourself back up again. To make this harder, move your hands further away from your knees.

Advanced option
Place hands shoulder width apart with your feet on the floor, lower yourself until your chin nearly touches the floor. As with the beginner option, remember to keep your back straight by pulling your belly button up to your spine and clenching your buttocks.

situps

Lie on the floor with your knees bent and feet on the floor, place your hands either behind your head or across your chest. If you place your hands beside your head, remember to keep your elbows out to the side and your chin off your chest. Push your lower back into the floor and lift your upper body off the floor. Great for your abs.

pelvic tilt, standing

This one strengthens the lower abs. It's a bit tricky but worth the effort! Stand with your back against the wall, pull your belly button into your spine and try to flatten the arch in your lower back. Keep your body nice and straight as you do this. Hold this for 10 seconds and breathe normally.

back extension

Lie on your stomach and place your hands under your chin. Keeping your legs and feet on the ground, slowly lift your upper body until your chest comes off the floor, then lower. NB Lower back exercises should be done slowly and gradually – no jerking movements.

dips

Beginner's option

Get a chair and sit on the very edge. Place your hands on the edge of the chair, shoulder width apart. Have your feet flat on the floor with your knees bent at 90 degrees. Keep your body straight as in the push ups, pulling your belly button onto your spine. Take your weight onto your hands and lower your bum to the floor. If this is too easy move your feet further away from the chair.

Advanced option

Arrange two chairs as in the picture, place your hands shoulder width apart and place your feet on the other chair Lower your body keeping your back straight and your stomach muscles tight.

Photos: Mike Searle

alternate arm leg raises

Lie on your stomach and slowly raise your right arm and left leg at the same time then do the opposite sides left arm and right leg. If you experience any pain STOP. Great for your lower back.

Just remember to take it easy in your first couple of weeks and don't over do it. If you get any pain, please STOP and go and see your doctor. These exercises should not cause you any pain if you are doing them correctly.

Turning up the Heat

OK, you've mastered the basics. Now it's time for the big girl's stuff.

shoot for the moon even if you miss you will land amongst the stars - Jill McLemore, writer

Turning up the heat

getting to your feet in the surf

To catch a wave, paddle hard and as you feel the tail of the board lift get ready to stand up. The first thing to do is push up with your arms. At the same time, slide the knee of your back leg up the board. Make sure that it is positioned in the centre of the board. Keep your weight forward leaning through your shoulders. Focus on keeping your head up, this will keep the nose of your board up and stop you from nose diving. As you gain momentum, bring your front foot forward and place it in the middle of the board.

Keep your balance in this drop knee position by holding your arms out to your sides like a tight-rope walker to help keep your balance. Your front foot should then be brought through and placed in the middle of the board just forward of the centre point. Don't stand up bolt upright, again keep a low centre of gravity. Your body should be kept sideways and you should be looking forward, keeping your nose roughly in line with your knee and your foot. As you become better at this technique you should begin to try the first technique as jumping straight to your feet will make steeper drops easier.

Once you've finished your ride, don't just run up onto the sand as this will more than likely snap your fins. Just step off the side of the board and you will stop. Never dive off! This maybe difficult at first but don't worry it's all part of learning a new skill.

bodyboarding

In order to get used to the waves and catch plenty of rides quickly, many girls choose to give bodyboarding a try. Just grab a suitably sized board (one that reaches your belly button when it's stood in front of you), get a pair of swim fins (flippers) and go for it. Any kind of waves can be ridden, the board is soft so you don't have to worry about being hit by it and it's smaller and lighter so it's easier to lug around. Within a few sessions you should be proficient to paddle out into the line up and catch unbroken waves and 'trim' along.

The sport is hugely popular with girls in Brazil, Hawaii and Australia, it offers easily achievable goals quickly as it's easier to keep your balance while at the same time offering a great sensation of speed when you're riding because you are closer to the wave. Check out the ThreeSixty Bodyboard Manual for more information about the sport, available from www.orcashop.co.uk

paddling out

Intermediates will want to go further out to sea than waist depth and this involves paddling...and the realisation that you need to develop a completely new set of shoulder muscles! To paddle your board, lie on it so the board's nose is just clear of the surface of the water. Paddle using a swimming 'crawl' stroke and keep your head up to see where you're going. After 10 minutes of this you'll probably be in agony! The reason for this is that you don't yet have strong enough back and shoulder muscles to maintain the paddling action. But don't worry, you'll develop them in time. A few lengths of the local pool will also help.

Paddling out through line after line of whitewater is hard work. Advanced surfers use a technique called duck-diving to get under the waves (see next page), but beginners' boards are too buoyant. Instead you need to paddle hard towards the wave, shift your weight back so the nose of the board lifts up just before the wave reaches you, then let the wave pass underneath you.

With practise, you'll find that the key to paddling is to use a steady rhythm. Don't paddle flat out, go at a steady pace. Save some energy for the occasional burst of speed that you'll need to get over a big set.

waxing your board

An essential ingredient to your pre-surf preparations, a thin layer of wax applied to the deck of the board gives you grip and will stop you from slipping off.

Alex Williams

ESTPIX

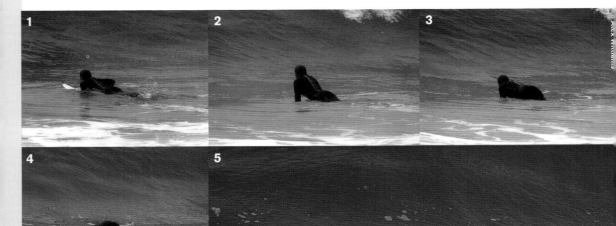

1
2
3
4
5
6
7

duck diving
by Kay Holt

Step One

To get through oncoming waves, you'll have to make the decision to go over or go under them. To go over them there are two techniques.

1. Paddle as fast as you can, as it gets close 1.5m-2m from you, lean back, lift the nose and let the wave glide past underneath you, holding onto the board otherwise it may hit you in the face.

2. If you have mastered the first technique, and find that you get pushed back too far as you go over, try stopping, sinking your board by sitting on it, then when the wave is 2-3m from you, release the board and use the boards buoyancy to propel you over the foam.This is great fun on a longboard.

Step Two

If it is too big to go over (i.e you get pushed over and back to shore by the force of the wave) then the turtle turn is the next option. Paddle hard, when the foam is 1.5-2m away, grab the rails and roll the board over. Then let the foam roll over your board. When you re-surface, kick and roll back up and get on your board again quickly. Start paddling again.

Step 3

If the whitewater is too big or a wave is about to break on top of you, then you need to 'duckdive' i.e. go under the wave. Again get the speed up, slide your hands up and push your body forward, then push the board under the water (by doing a press up). As the nose sinks get your knee on the back of the board and shove the tail down. This should force the board's nose to lift and as you get the turning right, you'll soon pop up through the back of the wave. Start paddling again.

Step 4

In bigger surf, you need to paddle faster towards the wave, duck dive earlier and stay 'tucked in' for longer before you come up.

Finally, the key to getting out the back quickly is timing. Try to paddle out when you see that a set has almost finished breaking, then use the channels (the flat water areas) and paddle as hard as you can. Watch out for rip currents – paddle sideways out of them, never against them. And remember practice makes perfect!

catching green waves

So now you're out in the lineup, ready to catch some green (unbroken) waves. Before going for one, spend a few minutes watching where the other surfers are taking off and how the waves are breaking. Don't paddle for closeouts; go for waves which are peeling. Remember to look both ways along a wave before paddling for it as another surfer may already be up and riding. Remember the drop-in rule: the surfer nearest the curl has right of way.

The technique for catching green waves is the same as before, except that you need to get to your feet quicker and keep your balance as you drop down the face of the wave. Lean forward, keep your head up and back arched or you'll pearl (dig the front of the nose). Remember, your front foot is the accelerator and your back foot is the brake.

taking the drop

Whether two feet or six feet the principles behind the most important of all surfing manoeuvres remains the same. After making sure you have enough paddling speed to catch the wave smoothly and get to your feet, you should shift your weight slightly forward onto your front foot, focussing on the wave face looking for any lumps or bumps that may trip you up on the way down. Your angle of descent should be adjusted depending on the steepness of the wave and the approaching section. The trick to pulling off late drops is confidence. If you go hard and strong you are more likely to drive down the wave face than hesitating at the top and falling off the back of the wave, or worse still getting dragged over the falls! Aim to go from prone position (lying down) to your feet in one smooth flowing movement, move quickly and fluidly and you will have a better chance of keeping your balance.

If the nose of your board starts to go under, shift your weight to your back foot slightly, this should raise it and avert disaster.

LAYNE BEACHLEY PERFORMS A TEXT BOOK BOTTOM-TURN.

basic turns

Okay, so you've paddled out and even caught a green wave. (How much fun was that?) But that's just the start, now it's time for the really fun bits, turning, throwing spray, carving and styling.

Forehand bottom to top turns

Your first turn will probably be on your forehand, or facing the wave. This is because it's easier to see, and the natural way you'll want to go. The first manouvre to master is the bottom turn. This is the basis of all good surfing.

Start by paddling and catching the wave. Jump to your feet and head down the wave so you make the drop to the bottom. Now to go in the required direction look, and point your leading arm where you want to go while leaning into the wave slightly and applying pressure on your inside rail. Your weight will be mainly on your toes.

Don't lean too far at first, just go gently. Chances are you'll lean without pushing hard enough with your toes and and fall flat on your face. Don't worry, everyone does it at first. If you push too hard you may fly off the back of the wave. Just relax and try to feel the water rushing up the wave face and the way it affects the board.

Now push the board back into a trim (horizontal position). With the effect of the turn, and the water moving up the wave, you have to push the board back down otherwise you will just topple over the back of the wave. Remember, drop, look, point and lean, then push back down.

After you've done a few of these you'll be flying along the face and at sometime you'll want to turn back into the wave or quite sharply down the wave face. Again, look where you want to go, turn your head, shoulders and point where you want to go with your arm, but this time apply your weight to the heel of your back foot while guiding the board with the heel of your front foot. It's a bit like standing on one leg while moving the other.

The theory behind turns is that if you look and point your head, shoulders and hips will follow. Don't worry if you fall, everyone does. Just keep at it and it will come.

If you have pulled off the move you'll find yourself back at the bottom of the wave. Now repeat the bottom turn and hey presto, you're ripping!

surviving wipeouts

The ability to survive wipeouts is the defining factor in a surfer's life. If you're not afraid and have the knowledge and fitness to survive them, the world is your oyster.

Of course, any wipeout means that you're going to go underwater and get rolled about a bit. Understanding this process is the key to overcoming your fear. Ask anyone if they could jump in the swimming pool and hold their breath for 30 seconds and most would give it a go without a second thought. However 30 seconds under a wave seems like a very long time. The washing-machine like turbulence is the thing that brings out fear. You can't see, you feel overpowered and it's these two things that are frightening.

ROCHELLE BALLARD DEMONSTRATES THE OCCUPATIONAL HAZARDS OF BEING ONE OF THE WORLD'S MOST FEARLESS WOMEN SURFERS.

The thing to remember is the kind of wipeouts that most of us will face actually don't go on for very long, they just feel like it! Most wipeouts last for about 10 seconds. If you can hold your breath for 30, then this is no big deal, is it? So once you have this in your head, the most important thing to do is relax and let the energy disperse and wait for the wave to pass over. You can't fight it anyway, so you may as well just chill and let it happen. In bigger waves it's slightly different, but we'll look at that later.

If you feel yourself losing balance, try to wipeout safely by jumping away from your board, preferably behind it. Never dive off head-first in shallow water unless you want to spend the rest of your life in a wheelchair. If there's a danger of your board hitting someone else, try to hold onto it. When re-surfacing from a wipeout always protect your head by covering the back of your neck with one arm, and your crown and face with the other.

SHAUNA WARD PERFORMING HER BACKHAND BOTTOM TURN.

backhand bottom-turns

Turning backhand, or with your back to the wave, is slightly scary when you're first setting out, but it's no different than going forehand apart from you have to look over your shoulder.

Okay, so same deal, paddle, stand and drop. Now look and point. Your leading arm will now be pointing behind your body and up onto wave. If you try this now while sitting down you'll feel how this action opens your shoulders and drags your hips around. When you're on the wave this will transfer your weight onto your heels and you'll be leaning into the wave slightly. Again it is perfectly normal to feel like you're falling over backwards and fall on your bum. Even six-times world champ Layne Beachley would have done it at some point. It's the same as doing a forehand cutback but slightly easier as the water rushing up the face will help turn your board for you.

Getting back down is also easier as you are now facing where you want to go and can see everything more clearly. The backhand off-the-top is exactly the same in principle as your first bottom turns except you're heading down the wave, not up. So: look, point and apply weight to your toes.

Once you're down the bottom again repeat the bottom turn. Now we're surfing!

The anatomy of a cutback

pressure on heels

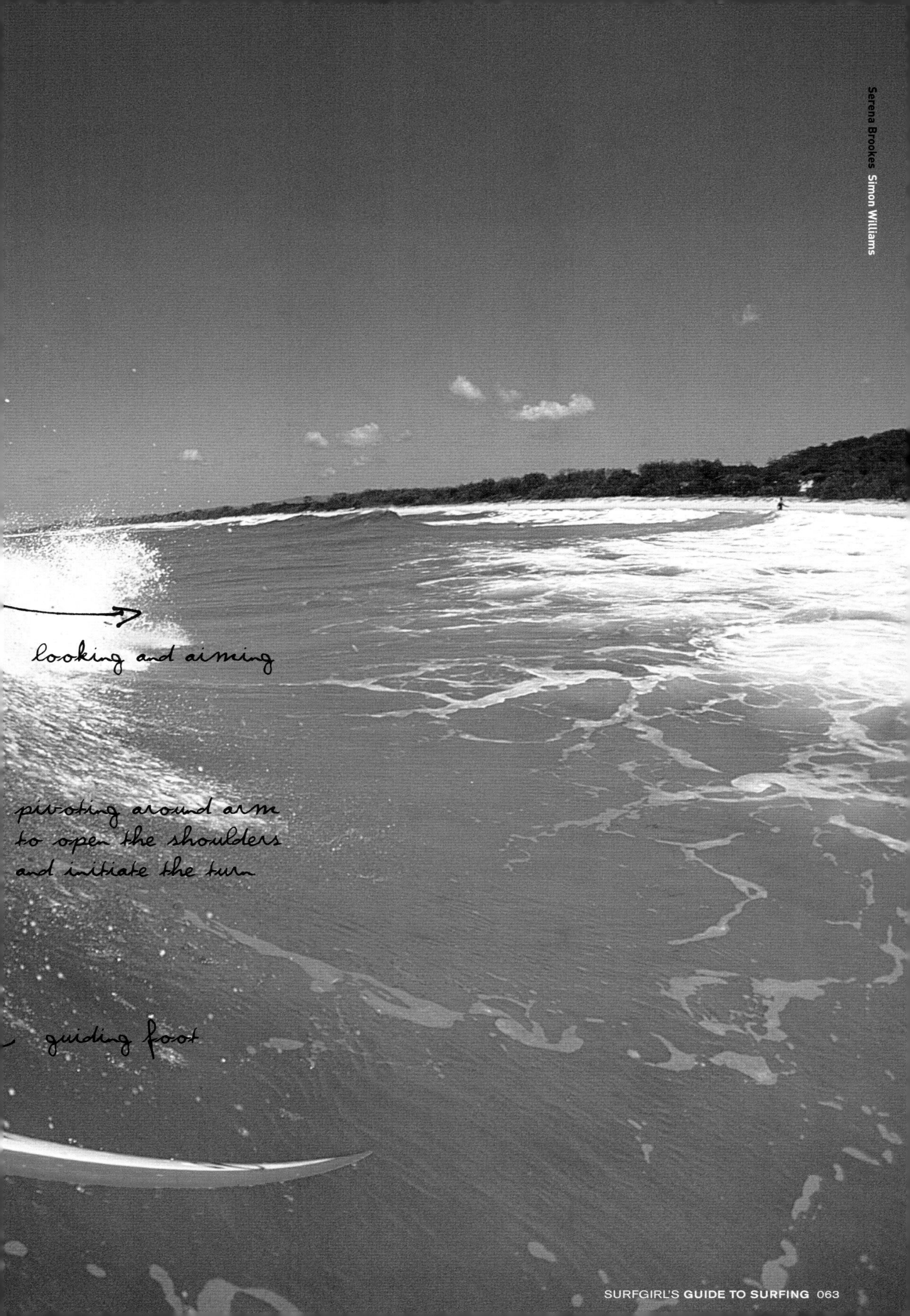

looking and aiming
pivoting around arm
to open the shoulders
and initiate the turn
guiding foot

Serena Brookes Simon Williams

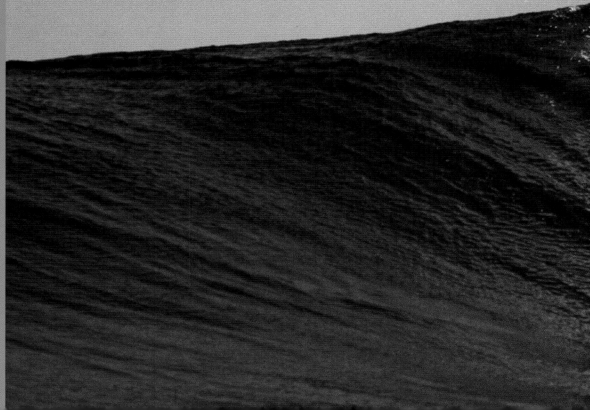

Tearing it up

Congratulations, you're a hottie! Here's the stuff that's going to impress folks on the beach. Just find the sweet spot on the wave and blow up.

your dreams can be realities they are the stuff that leads us through life toward great happiness

- Deborah Norville, writer

Tearing it up

Sequence: Simon Williams

roundhouse cutback

This basic manoeuvre enables the surfer to change direction and return to the steepest part of the breaking wave, the pocket, without loss of speed. There are several varieties of cutbacks, from simple carves to full figure-of-eight manoeuvres ('roundhouse cutbacks'); the type you can perform will depend on the wave's shape and power. Small mushy waves require small snappy cutbacks to retain maximum speed. Large powerful waves allow the surfer to go way out onto the shoulder, then accelerate through a large powerful turn back into the pocket, before slashing back around onto the wave face.

Here's Sam Cornish performing a nice sweeping version. The key points to note are that she's looking around towards the pocket (so her shoulders and torso also turn, and guide her board around), and she's using her outside arm as the pivot point on which to base the turn.

Sequence: Simon Williams

floater

The floater re-entry, one of the hottest moves of the '80s, is now a standard manoeuvre for most advanced surfers. The basic floater is performed by steering your board up onto the breaking lip with enough speed to glide along it for some distance, before dropping down the curtain of the wave and continuing the ride. Floaters, like aerials, are 'horizontal' manoeuvres: you set them up by pumping down the line, doing a shallow bottom-turn, and gliding up onto the lip at maximum speed. Then it's just a matter of committing yourself and steering out of the lip, so that you freefall back down into the trough of the wave. In this sequence Chelsea Georgeson floats out with the lip and into freefall mode.

Forehand snap

The vertical top turn is a more critical version of the basic top turn, performed on the steepest section of the wave. To set up the manoeuvre you need to do a good wide bottom-turn, then project your board vertically up the wave face, aiming at the steepest part of the unbroken lip. As you reach the apex of the turn, twist your head and shoulders towards the bottom of the wave, and your board will follow suit, snapping tightly off the top. (Again, look towards the pocket of the wave, not at your board.) As you drop down the wave again, you'll pick up momentum for the next manoeuvre.

Here's four times Trudy Todd cranking a turn in Indonesia.

Sequence: Simon Williams

Sequence: Simon Williams

Sequence: Simon Williams

Backhand off-the-lip

As Sam Cornish shows here in Western Australia, the key to a good strong backhand off-the-lip begins with the bottom-turn. Open your body shape by pulling your inside shoulder towards the wave and look to the point you want to hit. As your shoulders turn whip the board through with your legs and re-adjust your weight onto your back foot. About three-quarters up the wave face you should feel ready to head back down — turn your head and shoulders back down the wave face and whip the board back under your body. The amount of spray you throw is directly related to the power you put into the snap back down.

TIP: Take aim! Look where you want to go. It sounds weird but whatever direction you're head is pointing in, the shoulders and then the rest of the body will follow.

Tailslide

Another of surfing's most radical manoeuvres, the tailslide is the result of a surfer hurtling into a top turn with so much power that the fins and tail of his board break free, and the rider slides through 90, 180, or even 360 degrees, before reconnecting and continuing his ride. Again, sucky three to five-foot beachbreak waves provide the ideal conditions.

To pull a tailslide, jam a bottom-turn at maximum speed and head for the lip (or oncoming foamball at the end of a section). As you hit the lip and your board begins to snap around, shift your weight onto your front foot and give the tail a good shove with your back foot. (This is one occasion when you do want to look at the tail of your board for a moment, as you don't want to set up a turning movement just yet.) As your fins break free and the board slides for a second or two, try to stay as low and centred as possible, and get ready for the fins to 'catch' and regain your forward momentum. This shot of Sam Cornish pulling a stylish tailslide left shows how important it is to have a low centre-of-gravity.

Simon Williams

Aerial

Aerials, or 'airs', are perhaps the most dynamic and impressive of all surfing manoeuvres. At top speed the surfer uses the natural curve of the wave as a ramp to blast upwards into the air, before landing back on the wave. Fast steep waves in the three to five-foot range (such as sucky shorebreaks) provide ideal ramps. Light cross-shore winds can also help. Look for a sucky section with a nice lip or a foamball coming towards you. Pump your board to gain maximum speed. Set up the manoeuvre with a mid-face turn (rather than a wide bottom-turn), keeping the board flat to the wave face. As you hit the lip, unweight your front foot and guide the nose of the board upwards and slightly shorewards, while giving the tail a kick (like a skateboarding ollie) with your back foot. You should now be in mid air! At this point you want to be in a compact, balanced position so you can control the board and prepare for landing. That's the theory anyway, and here's Claire Bevilacqua with a huge demonstration! On landing, try to absorb the impact by bending your knees, then just hang on. Airs are particularly difficult manoeuvres to master and you can do a fair bit of damage to yourself, your board, and other surfers in the process...so be careful!

Tube Ride

The tube ride is the ultimate surfing thrill, and has probably provided surfers with more conversational pieces over the years than chocolate, shopping or anything else you can think of!

Waves that tube are comparatively rare. They only occur when a clean powerful swell hits a shallow sandbar or reef, and the wave has so much power that the lip pitches out to form a tube. These kind of waves are always steep and powerful, so only advanced surfers are going to be able to catch them and make the drop. After that, the best advice we can give is to set your line, relax, and enjoy the ride!

Once you've got used to the initial sensation of tube-riding, you can try to increase your time in the tube by accelerating or decelerating as necessary. To slow down and stay inside for longer, try sticking your inside hand in the face of the wave. If you need to accelerate to make the section, shift your weight onto your front foot, or pump the board using your ankles and knees.

This sequence shows Sam Cornish tucked into a nice little tube in Australia. Note her low crouched body position, and the way she's using her inside hand to feel how close she is to the wave face.

Big waves and how to tackle them

With the new generation of up-and-coming rippers charging in the water, the constant challenge to go harder is driving girls into bigger and bigger surf. The keys to pushing your performance in bigger surf are fitness and building up your confidence. Even if you don't want to surf Waimea the following tips will help you push back your personal boundaries.

Perhaps the most important factor in surfing bigger waves is building confidence and changing one's perception of what is big and scary so you are comfortable in your new surroundings. It's all in the mind! Once you've experienced something, the sense of familiarity makes it all okay the next time you are in the same situation therefore you've overcome fear!

Physical fitness is really important. If your fitness is at a high level and you know you are capable of swimming a good distance, and holding your breath underwater without panicking, you'll feel pretty invincible. This is essential if you are going to paddle out and get onto a bomb! If you know you can deal with the consequences you won't be afraid of trying.

As we all know, it's hard doing exercise regularly, but if you manage a routine three to four times a week that should be enough. You'll find that 10-20 press-ups, sit-ups, burpees and lunges will do remarkable things for all aspects of your surfing. But remember you can go to the gym and swim a kilometre or two, but there is no substitute for getting in the water whatever the conditions. That's what will build your fitness, confidence and wave knowledge, giving you the edge.

● **To get out**, you have to be confident and you must power paddle when you see a gap opening up in the waves. After ducking through lots of white water, it helps if you kick as well

LAYNE BEACHLEY THE WORLD'S BEST SURF GIRL

as paddle. If a mother of a sucking monster is aiming to land on your head, try to stand on your board and dive for the sand and dig in or slide off early and try to swim as deep as possible.

● **When duckdiving,** speed really helps get you under the wave. Paddle hard for the final few strokes before you start to duck, then tuck your legs up as you go under as it creates less drag. Try to hang on to your board and not just trust your leash.

● **When paddling** for the wave, remember, once you commit yourself, it may be hard to pull back. Paddle with all you've got, even if you feel yourself going backwards up the wave. Give an extra stroke for luck, then get up in a crouch, so you

● **If you are going over the falls,** try get into a ball. This will help you penetrate the water, and lessens any chance of injury from either being hit be your board in vital areas, or bouncing off the bottom.

● **Never hesitate.** Whether paddling for a wave or getting to your feet, give it 100 percent. It sounds corny but hesitation really does make bad things happen! Once you've made a decision to go, do it!

● **Lastly, have fun** and smile when you make it to the beach. Give yourself a pat on the back and vow to take off on an even bigger one next time. Always remember that time honoured statement. "If you don't go, you won't know!" So go, enjoy the rush. **- Kay Holt**

Style and flow

LISA ANDERSEN — ALWAYS STYLISH

The two key elements that separate good surfers from very good surfers are style and flow.

If you watch a really good surfer they seem to gracefully fly along waves with maximum speed for minimum effort. They make it look easy. While we can't all be Layne Beachley there are things we can do that will help our surfing.

● **Make sure you spend time mastering the basics.** All good turns begin with the bottom-turn. It's the turn that sets up the whole wave. Try to draw smooth powerful lines.

● **Don't jump on a really short board too soon.** There is no surer way of destroying style. High volume boards give you the speed you need so you can concentrate on stylish turns. Low

volume boards often need the rider to generate speed and lead to intermediates desperately jumping up and down to achieve it. This looks terrible.

● **Use minimum body movement for maximum effect through turns.** It's no good waving your arms around as it doesn't really achieve anything. Try to bend your knees, staying low, and compact through bottom turns. This compresses your muscles like a spring until you are ready to push and burst into a turn.

● **Use your eyes and front arm as pointers.** Look and point where you want to go and your shoulders should follow taking your body through the turn. Try it out, it works!

● **Flow.** Remember waves are bundles of energy, so go with them not against them for maximum speed with minimum effort. Jumping up and down on your board won't make it go

faster, but putting it where the energy is and pumping it smoothly across the wave face will.

● **If you're going to snap, snap hard.** Getting to the top of the wave is only half of a re-entry, snap, or floater. Once you're up there you've got to get back down. Snapping down hard puts you board back under your feet and maintains the speed you need to get back down the wave face. Be positive!

● **Link sections.** Don't view a wave as a series of trick ramps, look down the line and try to read what the wave will do and which manoeuvres you need to maximise your speed through the whole ride. Your aim is to ride the wave to it's maximum potential.

● **If you get fed up, or feel a bit stale borrow a longer board and go and have fun.** Riding a longer board makes you put more effort into your turns which must be smoother and more drawn out. When you jump back onto your shorter board try to maintain the smooth flow.

● **Use footage from video cameras to check how you surf.** It's amazing how much you can learn. Even practising in front of the mirror at home to check your body positions through pretend turns can help.

● **Timing is everything,** whether it's being in synch with the ocean rhythms, or hitting the lip at the right time. Surf as much as you can, in all conditions. There is no substitute for water time.

- Kay Holt

Cruising

So you don't want to rip, slash and tear. That's okay... sometimes it's cool to go with the flow and cruise.

variety is the soul of pleasure

Aphra Behn, writer

Cruising

HAWAII'S MARY BAGALASO TAKES THE DROP ON A NINE-FOOTER.

Longboarding is more about elegance and grace than the faster, snappy manouvre-orientated style of shortboarding. These days, many longboard surfers are mixing classical and progressive modern-day manoeuvres to a create an exciting new approach to riding these traditional surf vehicles. UK longboard champ Dominique Munroe takes you through the differences between the two styles of short and longboarding and explains the manoeuvres.

differences between long and shortboards

The sheer lengths of these boards make surfing them a competely different discipline. On a shortboard a surfer can turn by simply leaning one way or the other with their feet firmly planted on one spot. But on a longboard a surfer has to use her weight and position on the board to make turns which are drawn out longer. To achieve a change of position on the board the surfer "walks the board", moving up and down its length.

The takeoff on a longboard is more relaxed because you can catch the wave sooner and it's not so important to be in the critical part of the wave. This is because the added flotation makes it much easier to catch the wave.

As longboards take more effort to turn, the takeoff is really important as it sets the surfer up for the best position on wave. You can slow the board down and use a "fade" takeoff or angle the board into the wave to speed it up and get through a fast section.

Overall, longboards are great for smaller days as having extra length and volume in the board helps to get over flat sections of the wave, which would see a shortboard struggling to maintain speed.

Simon Williams

Tara Moller

LOUISE WEST ON THE NOSE.

beginner

A mini-mal (7'0" to 8'0" in length) is an ideal learning board for a beginner. The extra length, thickness and width make paddling and catching waves so much easier. Having a thicker, wider board also plays a big part in helping the learner as the extra width makes the board more stable and standing up a lot less wobbly!

All these factors help immensely when you are a beginner making the learning process much easier and faster than if you started out on a shorter board. However, true longboards (over 9'0" in length) are not suitable for beginners as they're unweildy and too much of a handful to control.

Tara Moller

DOMINIQUE MUNROE HAVING FUN IN MOROCCO.

intermediate

takeoff

The fact that longboards are less responsive and take longer to turn means that getting the board in the best position on the wave has a lot to with the takeoff. Whether it's a fade take off (angling into the curl before bottom turning away and across onto the face) to set the board up ready for nose-riding or to gain speed through a fast section, mastering the takeoff is really important.

trim

This is where you position the board in the fastest part of the wave and get the board achieving its maximum speed. To do this, the surfer walks forward on the board to speed it up and to prevent it from stalling, or moves back towards the tail to slow the board down and stop it from nose diving.

cross stepping

Cross stepping is where the surfer walks the board by placing one foot across the other to gracefully move up and down the board. This is far more stylish than shuffling your feet up to the nose.

top and bottom turns

Turning a longboard is a lot harder than turning a shortboard. The sheer length, and the fact that you have more board in the water, means everything is slower and more drawn out. A surfer has to move towards the back of the board in order to manoeuvre the board around, pushing from the knees and swinging of the arms in the direction of the turn. A good longboarder will make this move look effortless.

Simon Williams

HANG FIVE!

cutback

A cutback is performed when the board has raced ahead of the breaking wave onto the flat section and naturally slows down. To re-position the board and regain speed, the surfer turns the board back towards the breaking part of wave, putting the board once more into the curl of the wave. The whole time a surfer is on a wave they are constantly positioning and repositioning themselves to ensure optimum speed.

kicking out

This is a controlled exit off the wave. It is performed by turning the board so it rides up and over the back of the wave by pushing down on the tail and lifting the nose over the wave face.

nose riding

The first 12 inches of the front of the board is considered to be the nose of the board. To get to the nose, a surfer has to first set up the board by keeping the tail of the board in the pocket of the wave, this ensures the tail is being held down by the volume of breaking water pushing down on it. This counter-balances the surfer's weight and allows them to cross-step quickly up to the nose without sinking the front end of the board. Making sure the inside rail is in the face of the wave also helps provide the stability to perform a good nose ride.

Simon Williams

BELEN CONNELLY PULLS IN

advanced

hanging five and ten

By taking the technique used for nose-riding a little further, the surfer cross-steps to the front of the board and places either five or ten toes over the front of the board. Grace and technique play a vital role in performing this manoeuvre with the style it demands.

off-the-lip

By turning the board and heading up to the top of the wave a surfer can get a large amount of the board out of the wave before swinging it back

down with the whitewater and continuing to trim a long the wave.

floater

This requires a fair amount of speed to initially drive the board up the wave, ride along on top of the breaking wave before plunging back down onto the face of the wave or the whitewater if the wave has closed out.

Whatever your age or ability, practice makes perfect, so the best advice to anyone is to feed the addiction and get out there as often as possible. Keep at it, longboarding is a hard sport to learn, but well worth it.

Body and soul

Surfing is a physical and spiritual artform. You'll need to nurture the mind as well as the body in order to achieve unity and balance in surfing and in life.

the secret of health for both mind and body is not to mourn for the past, not to worry about the future, or not to anticipate troubles, but to live in the present moment wisely and earnestly. - Buddha

Body care

Be at your best inside and out. Tackle those waves looking and feeling great by inventing your own health and beauty routine. Here's a pick'n'mix of great ideas.

Inside
wonder water

Surfers have a lot in common with the sea...our bodies are 70 percent water and the molecular formation of blood is close to that of seawater. So drink lots, especially in hot climates and if you're doing lots of exercise. Filtered water is best, or mineral water, or you could try Lucozade Sport Hydro active — water with vitamins and salts to replace fluid lost during exercise.

you are what you eat

If you put in rubbish, your body is not going to look or perform at its best. The right nutrition will also keep your complexion clear, your immune system in good shape and keep you surfing longer.

In these days of conflicting diet advice, just remember the basics: eat a balance of foods, at regular intervals, keeping meals as fresh and organic as possible: eat what's most natural to the climate you are in (i.e. eat what the locals eat) and try to avoid additives in food like E-numbers and colouring. Get fruity! Eat a minimum of five pieces of fruit or veg per day. Do not eat anything up to an hour before going into the water (resulting cramps can kill even strong swimmers).

detox

Even if you haven't been on a chips and beer diet, a detox is great for the skin and will re-vitalise your whole system by clearing out toxins which will in turn energise you. *Detox* by Penelope Sach is a pocket-sized Penguin book with 10 simple methods to follow. But generally, there are three foods to help rejuvenate your insides, they are alfalfa sprouts, avocado and garlic.

supplements

Try and get all your vitamin requirements by eating well. A general all-rounder if you are lacking energy is to take a slow release multi-vitamin like Quest Super Once A Day. Zinc is useful to ward off colds and promotes skin tissue healing. FSC make chewable flavoured lozenges.

Everybody is unique, so how do you know exactly which minerals your body is short of and which foods are best for you? To find out, Nutrition 4 All (020 8954 9995) will laboratory analyse a small sample of your hair. For £50 it's well worth it.

Outside

mud magic

A face pack is a treat for your skin, but make sure no one's there with a camcorder! Why not get every last bit of make-up out and try deep cleansing Cleopatra style? A Dead Sea mud mask will absorb impurities and replenish your skin's minerals for a radiant complexion. Ahava do a range at Selfridges or by mail order www.ahava.com.

exfoliate/cleanse/tone

Try these gentle and effective ideas for any skin types:

Mix 20 grams of bran and 20 grams of oats in a muslin bag, put it under a running tap when you're in the bath. Afterwards, rub the bag on your body — it's very softening for the skin and less drying than salt rubs.

For the face, try a tablespoon of olive oil mixed with a teaspoon of sugar. Apply in small circular movements with your fingers, rinse with warm water and tone with rose water.

Use your fingers rather than cotton wool with cleansers to avoid pulling the skin. Warm the cream in your hands first to make it more emollient and therefore more effective.

moisturising

There are hundreds to choose from, so choose one that is compatible to your skin and avoid those with 'fragrance' which means lots of chemicals.

Alternatively you could make your own by getting some base cream from your chemist and adding a drop of your favourite essential oils. To get the most from your beauty sleep, use night creams on your face.

love your pits

Do not use sprays or roll-ons directly after shaving. Anti-perspirants block the delicate underarm pores, so the kinder (and possibly safer) alternative is to go for a product which is deodorant only, like Tom's of Maine or Desert Essence.

facial workout

The facial muscles attach directly to the skin, so keeping them massaged and exercised with deliberate expressive stretches and contractions is likely to mean less sagging as you get older.

the mane attraction

Going in and out of the sea means extra care is needed on your follicles, so don't skimp on your conditioning. Leave-in spray conditioner is also fantastic for de-tangling and is useful on the go. Once in a while use a more intense treatment, especially if you have damaged or dyed hair. Always finish using cold water so the follicles 'close in' the conditioner. If you've got a hot date, see what happens when you add a few drops of sensual Ylang Ylang aromatherapy oil in your final rinse.

Yoga and surfing

Yoga has become one of the exercise regimes of the moment with just about every celeb sporting yoga clothes and swanning around with a yoga mat under their arms. Although it is easy to laugh at the stereotypes, yoga is here to stay and this is because it is an ancient programme of exercises that has been proven to work.

For surfers that are committed to keeping fit and therefore getting the most out of every session, yoga is an invaluable tool, as it will keep you in shape and flexible even when you can't get in the water. Yoga helps to improve your balance, focus, and breathing and will also realign your body after you have taken a pounding.

THE SURF GIRL CREW GOING THROUGH THEIR YOGA ROUTINE AT THE LANZAROTE TRAINING CAMP.

stretching out with Robyn Davies

I'm not very good, I'm not even very proficient at yoga, but it has helped me on so many different levels. From strengthening muscles I didn't even know were there to becoming as supple as I've ever been and helping me improve my surfing. What more can I say, it's ace! Try it, whatever path you're walking.

Mountain Pose
Stand upright, feet together, activating the bandhas (energetic relay); energise the legs, feet, arms and hands. Look straight ahead keeping the core of the body soft, with rhythmic Ujjayi (victorious, powerful) breathing.

Intense stretch pose
With the pelvis pivoted over the top of the thighs, feet alive, legs strong and straight, maintain the bandhas with the abdomen long hollow and empty, the chest broad and full, and lengthen the spine down the legs. Keep the core of the body soft with rhythmic Ujjayi breathing

The Cobbler
Sit with the feet in front of you, using your fingers and thumbs to open them like a book and use the grip of your hands and your arms to lengthen the spine. Clarify the bandhas with the abdomen long, hollow and empty, the chest broad and full, and soften the core of the body with smooth, rhythmic Ujjayi breathing.

Peggy Hall is a yoga teacher/surfer who has developed a series of yoga DVDs specifically for surfers. Here Peggy explains to **Jacqueline Wild** the benefits that yoga will have on your surfing.

What advantages would someone that practices yoga have over other surfers?

PH: Women who practice yoga will most likely have an advantage when they hit the water because they have already developed a keen sense of body awareness, which is essential to successful surfing. Yoga helps increase flexibility, strength, balance, lung capacity, endurance, and probably most important of all for surfing — mental focus. Surfing is all about being fully present in the moment and experiencing the body, mind, and spirit as one with the ocean!

I started to practice yoga a while after I started surfing, and I couldn't believe how much yoga helped improve my surfing! Most of all, I felt more confident in my body and my ability to handle whatever situation I was in. Most people new to surfing have moments of panic or fear in a wipeout, but yoga helps you learn to calm the mind and relax the body so even in a wipeout or heavy surf you can remain relaxed and focused.

Physically, yoga can really help improve balance, which is crucial for good surfing. Because yoga develops the small stabilising muscles that hug the bones, the larger muscles don't need to do all the work and

PEGGY HALL – YOGA GURU

so don't fatigue as quickly. Also, strong, supple muscles are less prone to injury and even protect bones from fracture. So, yoga helps prevent possible injuries from surfing and it's also great for strengthening the shoulders, back, and legs, all which are needed for fluid, powerful surfing!

Yoga very much emphasises breathing, which helps surfing in many ways. First, you can improve lung capacity and endurance (which helps with the long paddles back out). Yoga breathing gives you energy when you're fatigued and calms you when you're nervous. Yoga breathing also focuses the mind so you can concentrate on your relationship with the ocean and your ability to read the waves and surf without distraction.

What makes yoga such a good idea for surfers?

Yoga and surfing have a natural fit. Surfers want nothing more than to stay in the water as long as possible and to surf with as much energy and endurance as they can. Whereas most activities deplete energy, yoga actually restores energy by nourishing and revitalising every cell in the body! Most surfers want to improve their performance in the water as well as prevent and heal injuries. Yoga helps keep the body flexible, strong, balanced, and calm. Yoga is a perfect complement for surfing because it can be done as a pre-surf warm-up, a post-surf rejuvenation, and a conditioning workout when the surf is flat.

Yoga is renowned for its spiritual side – do you think that surfing also has a spiritual connection?

Yoga and surfing definitely share a spiritual connection! You see, yoga isn't just about flexibility - it's about awareness, about being totally alive in each moment, about finding a deep sense of well-being and inner strength by connecting the mind and body through the energy of the breath. Similarly, surfing is all about being one with the ocean, about tapping into the deep place inside where joy, bliss, and exhilaration reside. When you're surfing, you're totally in touch with creation! Any surfer knows the feeling of being

completely in the moment, connecting to the energy of the ocean and the power of the waves, challenging oneself to go beyond any self-limitations and to soar! This is ultimately what is so satisfying and addictive about surfing and yoga. That sense of oneness with nature is really what yoga — and surfing — is all about. Feeling joy from the depths of your soul!

For more surf-specific yoga poses, check out Yoga for Surfers 1 and 2 available from orcasurf.co.uk

Natural repair

Cheryl Davies

What's available for a girl with a board and a sens̶̶̶̶̶̶̶̶̶̶̶̶̶̶̶̶̶̶̶̶̶ likes to take a natural approach to health and healing? Rowena Wilson takes a look.

Complementary medicine and health products are becoming more and more popular and I've discovered plenty of useful items to take on surf trips that work really well. They are produced without harming animals or the environment and complement a well-sorted first aid kit and washbag.

aches and bruises

Hemp Zap Analgesic Balm (£7.99, thehempshop.net) is natural Deep Heat for sore and tired muscles. It smells better than conventional Deep-Heat too. Don't want an ugly bruise to form? **Arnica cream** (£4.95) is your best friend. If you collide with your board or somebody else's, rub it in straight after you come out of the water, before it has time to form. (NB Do not put on broken skin.)

cuts and infected wounds

Try **Tea Tree** (a rather smelly) oil for cuts, rashes, burns and blisters (at around £4). It's great to clean cuts and infected wounds and helps heal skin by encouraging the formation of scar tissue. It's a tiny but potent concentrated bottle, the size of a lipstick and will last ages. It's even good for acne, athlete's foot and is effective against cystitis and thrush and fighting colds and flu. (NB do not swallow.)

over-done it?

If you've had a heavy boozy night or indulged too much in strange, rich, fatty, spicy foods or coffee and only just lived to tell the tale and God forbid, next day can't even face the surf, then **Nux Vom homeopathic pill** may help you get on with your day (£3.50). If you needed to puke, it will help you clear it all out! Also used for constipation, diarrhoea and heavy menstrual bleeding.

diarrhoea

Alternative preparations are not designed to stop diarrhoea. If your body is trying to get rid of something in your guts at top speed, the theory is get rid of it, then rebuild your gut flora and immune system. If you must block it in, you'll need a conventional medicine to do it.

travel sickness

Chew **crystallised ginger** or try **Nelson's homeopathic Travella pills** (£4.20).

ears and eyes

These are much neglected areas. If you wear contact lenses, use daily disposables so that pollutants in the sea don't get a chance to grow bacteria on them that will transfer to your cornea and threaten your eyesight. For general eye soreness, try **Euphrasia Eye Tincture**. If you don't want to get surfer's ear (a bony growth in your ear canal) then use ear plugs, or put Blue Tac in your ears — roll it up into a small mushroom shape first. Earplugs can also save your ears from surfer's ear during the day and your nerves from being deprived of a night's sleep if walls are paper-thin.

insect stings

Nelson's Pyrethrum Spray (£4.20) is very portable and relieves the itch and discomfort of a bite or sting. Wearing **Citronella or lavender oil**, however, may help put the mosies off biting you to start with (around £4).

skin/hair

Martha Hill Deep Moisturising Conditioner with seaweed complex (£5.50) for dry and stressed hair and their **Evening Primrose and Lavender Body Oil** (£2.70 travel size) counteracts the drying effects of sun and salt water. (Tel; 0800 980 6662)

general help

Bach's Rescue Remedy (£3.95) goes everywhere with me. A few drops on the tongue are helpful after any kind of shock; accidents, emotional traumas or bad news. If you've been half-drowned, got whiplash from a hair-raising coach journey, chased by a raging bull or been chucked by your boyfriend, let its magic go to work.

Mark Mayell's book *Natural First Aid* **(Vermilion)** won't easily fit in your rucksack, but will give you more ideas of what to take and show you acupressure points for pain relief and so on before you go.

complete kits and specialist products

If you are lucky enough to be going to tropical climates, Helios homeopathic pharmacy supplies a kit called **Specifics for the Traveller** (£38.95), preparing you for everything from dysentery to cholera. Even if you are fully vaccinated and carry a whole armoury of medicines with you, this little box is certainly a wonderful bonus and contains clear info on how to use it. I always take mine abroad. (Helios tel; 01892 537254) Pure mail order products have a range of aromatherapy products, blended to order, with surfers in mind. These include soothing skin, hair and muscle care and bath oils to get you thoroughly refreshed and ready for more action. (Pure Tel 01903 879940).

All of these items complement a good first aid kit and common sense. Like all medicines, read the labels carefully before use (or get professional advice) and do not combine with alcohol — mainly because it inhibits the benefits. Homeopathic preparations, aromatherapy oils and Bach remedies are available in many chemists and health stores.

Environment and Surfing

One of the joys of surfing is that you get to experience a whole new perspective on this beautiful planet. The UK's coastline is rich with wildlife, and while waiting for waves you may get to see something like a seal or dolphin which will make your surfing even more memorable. So what can you see and how can we as surfers help to maintain this precious resource?

dolphins

There is something about spotting a dolphin that simply makes the heart sing. Dolphins are basically a coastal species and so your chances of spotting them are pretty good. Their inquisitive and playful nature means that they are also quite likely to make themselves known to you, by swimming underneath your surfboard and sometimes taking off on waves next to you.

Unfortunately dolphins are under threat due to pair trawling for sea bass, and sightings of dead dolphins or porpoises on the beach occur distressingly often. Greenpeace and local wildlife trusts like the Cornwall Wildlife Trust are campaigning to put an end to this needless killing and are compiling evidence that will help to get pair trawling banned. If you want to make your voice heard on the subject, Greenpeace have made this easy for those with internet access, as you only need to put your name to a ready made letter.

seals

Seals may never have been the star of their own TV show like Flipper, but their resemblance to Labrador pups with those big brown eyes, certainly makes them very appealing. Grey seals are extremely common along the UK's coastline and if you surf regularly, then your chances of seeing one or more are very good. Britain is home to two-thirds of the world's population of seals and they can be seen predominantly in Scotland, Cornwall and the Scillies, the Pembrokeshire islands, the Farne islands and the north and west coasts of Ireland.

However if you encounter a seal pup on the shore then leave it alone, as you might scare it, or it's mother, if you interfere. If it looks as though it is in trouble phone The National Seal Sanctuary on 01326 221361, or your nearest RSPCA officer.

sharks

Sharks are probably one of the most feared inhabitants of the ocean and the film *Jaws* helped to increase paranoia on the subject. Although scientists reassure us that sharks do not mean to attack humans, this does not help those unfortunate enough to be the victim of mistaken identity, like 13-year-old surfer Bethany Hamilton, who suffered an attack in Hawaii when her left arm was bitten off.

The UK has long been seen as a safe zone in terms of dangerous creatures, but there are nevertheless 28 species of shark around the UK, including blue, spurdogs, basking, threshers, porbeagle, tope and dogfish. The World Wildlife fund reports that there are between 30 - 70 million shark deaths a year due to a trade in skin and meat, which is threatening the survival of some species. Although sharks don't have the appeal that dolphins do, their survival is essential for the health of the ocean, as a massive reduction in numbers will result in the ocean's ecosystem becoming imbalanced.

basking sharks

Basking sharks are the second largest fish in the world, sometimes reaching 12 metres in length and seven tonnes in weight. Their dorsal fins can protrude two metres out of the water, which could be enough to make you panic and swim for shore, but thankfully basking sharks are plankton eaters with no interest in humans.

Basking sharks are most likely to be seen along the Cornish coast (and perhaps Scotland) in June, but they follow the patterns of plankton availability and can therefore be spotted from spring through to autumn.

turtles

It seems hard to believe, but turtles can actually be spotted in the UK. Leatherback turtles are the largest living turtles, with one record-breaking male being measured at 2.6 metres after he was found stranded in Wales. These endangered creatures swim from their breeding grounds in the Caribbean to feed on jellyfish in British shores.

The Marine Cornwall Society is tracking information on jellyfish, since this is the primary source of food for Leatherbacks and are encouraging people to report their sightings. The MCS is providing people with a jellyfish identification kit in order to help and you can get this free by emailing peter@mcsuk.org or calling 01989 566017.

jellyfish

Jellyfish are incredible and beautiful creatures, in or out of the water, but the fact that they can give you a bit of a sting is enough to make you be wary of them. Thankfully their stings are not able to penetrate a wetsuit and so if you find yourself close to one, then it is probably best to keep any exposed areas away from the tentacles. Putting your face in the water for a better look is definitely not a good idea! If you do get stung by a jellyfish, then it is recommended that you treat it with cold packs for 10 – 15 minutes. If the sting does not subside then you should see a doctor.

weaver fish

Weaver fish are pesky little critters that submerge themselves in the sand to spawn during the summer months. They have venomous and spiny backs which when trodden on will feel like a nasty bee sting. The venom is de-activated by heat and many local cafes will sympathetically provide you with a 'weaver bucket' filled with hot water to help alleviate the pain.
- Jacqueline Wild

useful websites

World Wildlife Fund www.wwf-uk.org/core/index.asp
Cornwall Wildlife Trust www.cornwallwildlifetrust.org.uk
Whale and Dolphin Conservation Society www.wdcs.org
Greenpeace's new ocean site www.greenpeace.org.uk/oceans
Seal Sanctuary www.sealsanctuary.org
Surfers Against Sewage www.sas.org.uk
Marine Conservation Society www.mcsuk.org

a healthy ocean

When you surf, it is hard to ignore the beauty around you and the importance of maintaining this is essential for your continued happiness in the water. Pollution is a major threat to ocean health, as chemicals can alter the physiology and reproduction of invertebrates and fish, as well as causing algae to grow, which can potentially kill a wide range of ocean dwellers.

The major source of ocean pollution comes from agricultural waste and sewage (about 70%) and Surfers Against Sewage are prominent in their commitment to clean seas. SAS believe that there are alternative ways of treating waste and that instead of simply dumping it into the ocean, it could potentially be recycled and used on the land.

More than two billion sanitary items are flushed down UK toilets every year, including tampons and condoms, which contribute to the pollution levels in the oceans. If you are concerned about this, then it is important to remember to bin such items, rather than flushing them down the toilet.

Other ways that you can help include:
• **Buy organic** – organic produce is grown with greater sensitivity to the land and will help reduce farm related waste.
• **Buy eco friendly products** – everything from washing-up liquid to toothpaste, will eventually make it back to the ocean and so it is important to use products that have a low environmental impact.
• **Support SAS and WWF**, who are doing their best to make sure that the ocean and its inhabitants remain healthy.

Sun seduction

How you look after yourself in the sun is vital especially if you're out in it all day as excessive exposure can take its toll on your body. But you can still get that dreamy summer look, and some lovely vitamin D, if you are willing to get gently sun-kissed and not sun-snogged!

Be sun aware

Build your tan slowly. If the swell is fantastic the first day you arrive and it's 90° in the shade, try and resist it al least until the sun is past its peak.

• **Apply sunscreen** 20 minutes before going out, to allow absorption.

• **Be generous in your applications** — a thin cover will diminish your protection.

• **Expose your skin in small doses** and apply high factor sunscreen every one to two hours.

• **Don't forget** your nose, hands and ears or the backs of knees and soles of the feet if you are lying downwards.

• **Always re-apply after being in the water**, whatever the product claims. Laboratory tests suggest that 80 minutes is the longest waterproof products remain effective.

• **Use factor 30 for chest and face** and 15 for the rest of your body.

• **Use a PABA-free sunscreen**, this chemical could cause irritation and stain clothing.

• **Pile on the moisturiser afterwards.**

• **Some essential oils are damaging in the sun.**

• **Use a product on your forehead that won't drip** into your eyes and be a pain whilst your surfing or sweating. Sticks are more wax based, so are heavier and don't tend to run. Some (like ProSport) won't stick to sand either.

• If you've had a lot of exposure over the years already, **get regular checks at the docs.** Early detection of a melanoma may save your life.

• **Cloudy skies can still let in 80% of UV** rays, so you need to be careful even when the sun isn't seducing you directly. Hide your hide under tightly woven fabrics that don't let those rays through.

• **A hat** won't just look good it will protect your scalp and your hair.

• **Polarised sunglasses are a must,** unless you want a constant squint and diminishing eyesight. There are so many cool styles that it's great they count as essential purchases.

• **Cover up** if you're out between 11am and 3pm. You'll never catch a supermodel sunbathing then. If you're surfing without a wetsuit at those times, consider a rash vest and shorts. (This will also help protect you from the where's-my-bikini-panic after wiping out!) — Rowena Wilson

Cheryl Davies

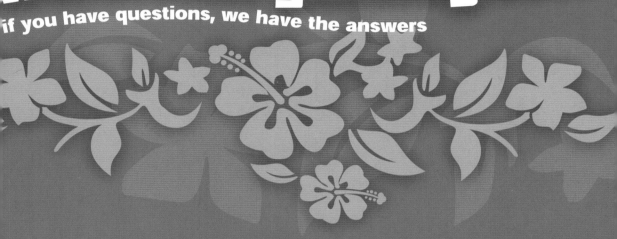

Locations: British Isles

Locations

Surfing in Britain can be testing at times, with abundant flat spells and a wide continental shelf which slows down open-ocean swells it's sometimes difficult to find good waves. That's why scoring great surf becomes so much more rewarding. With the advent of accurate surf prediction websites and weather models it's easier than ever to get to the right spot on the right day at the right time. Read on for some of the best spots the UK. We suggest beginner, intermediate and advanced spots in each area and also highlight the other major surfing zones that are worth exploring.

For more detailed information on these breaks check out the beach guide on the SurfGirl website. Go to surfgirlmag.com, for a comprehensive guide to the main surf spots in the UK plus you can check out the surf in the area on the daily updated surfcams. Also the Stormrider Guide to Europe is well worth a look, you can buy it online at surfgirlmag.com.

A T L A N

O C E A

2

3

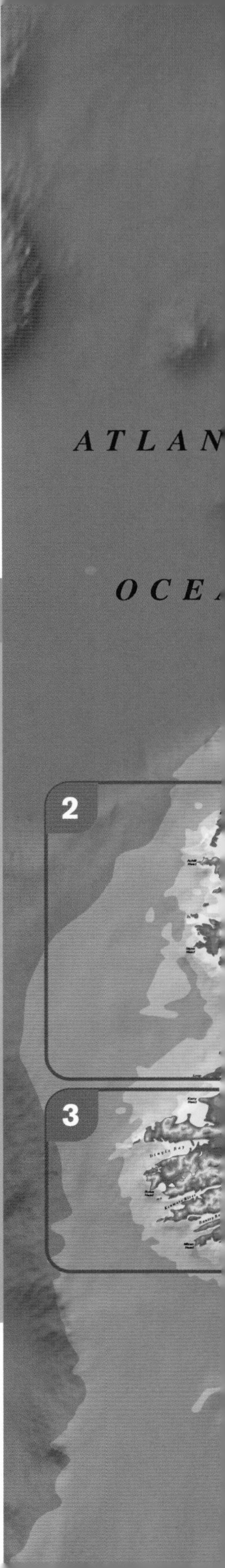

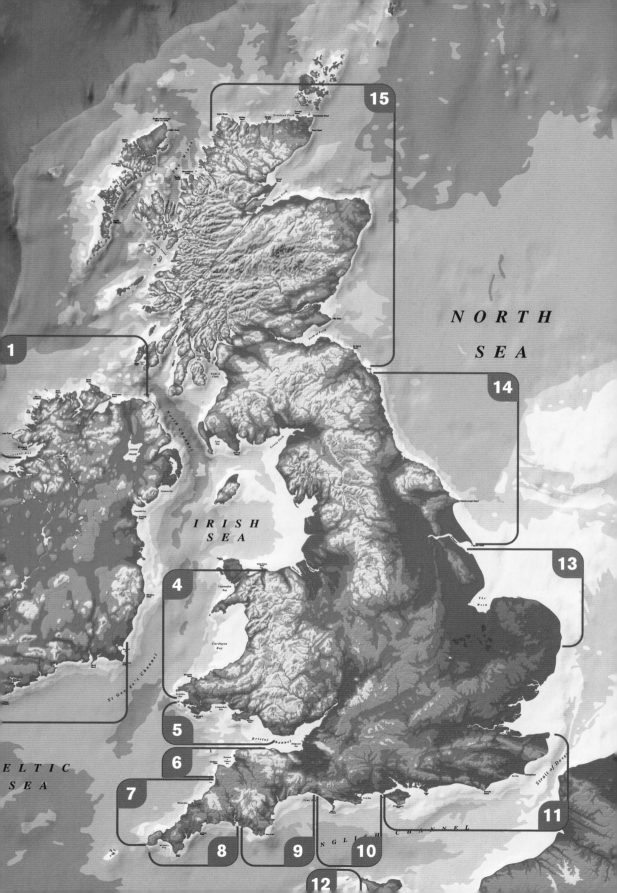

NORTH
SEA

IRISH
SEA

CELTIC
SEA

1

4

5

6

7

8

9

10

11

12

13

14

15

Ireland

If there is a deep low centred near Iceland, the west and north coasts of Ireland will pump. This place has got it all, making for endless potential. The island is divided into three main surfing areas; the Causeway Coast in Northern Ireland; Northwest Ireland from Bundoran to Easky, and Western Ireland from County Clare to the Dingle Peninsular. Check out these hot spots in the North West.

SOME DAYS, IT WOULD SEEM THAT THE ENTIRE COAST OF IRELAND IS BLESSED WITH PERFECT WAVES.

Beginner
Strandhill, Co Sligo
The waves at Strandhill beach are generally mellow especially in the summer. The main advantage of Strandhill is that it rarely goes flat, even if everywhere else is! This is mainly due to its geographical situation, which has a large swell window. The ideal wind direction is south east, which blows straight offshore. Strandhill works on all tides and is safest on a high tide.

Intermediate
Easky, Co Sligo
Easky consists of two main breaks, Easky Left and Easky Right. The Left is a long, slightly fat pointbreak, while the right is fast and quite hollow. Easky handles a variety of winds, and tides are not a major factor. The left is offshore on a southwest wind while the right needs an east wind. A north swell will get the left cranking while a slightly more west swell is better for the right. Summer flatness is a problem here, but for the rest of the year it's fairly consistent.

Advanced
Bundoran, Co Donegal
The Peak in Bundoran is one of the most testing waves in the country. The wave comes out of very deep water and meets the triangular shaped reef resulting in a perfect peak formation. It works for only two hours either side of low tide. The left is long and throws a barrel after take off, the right is much shorter but hollower. It needs a west swell and east winds to be perfect and can handle up to ten feet but rarely gets over four foot in the summer months.

THERE ARE PLENTY OF SECRET GEMS TO BE FOUND IN IRELAND.

Wales

Wales has a lot to offer all types of surfers , with a wide variety of waves from gentle beaches to gnarly reef-breaks. The biggest and best waves come alive during the winter months, when gales blow and lots of sheltered points and bays really turn on.

Phil Holden

OFFSHORE WAVES AT LLANGENNITH

Beginner
Rest Bay, Porthcawl
Rest Bay is perfect for a beginner since it's a long sandy beach which is easily accessible from low-to-high tide. It boasts about a mile of good surfable waves for all standards, but it's especially good for beginners since you can always find an area on the beach which is uncrowded so you can learn at your own pace, and try manoeuvres without the worry of hitting anyone. Rest Bay also has very few rips, which is a great peace of mind for beginners, and the waves which come through are both lefts and rights and are not especially heavy.

Intermediate
Langland, Swansea
Langland has a range of good waves – a reasonably heavy beachbreak which can often throw a few barrels, a right hand pointbreak, and an outer 'A' frame peak. This beach is best surfed from low to mid tide, and the various breaks work at different stages of the tide. So it's great for intermediates to try their hand at different wave conditions – but still with the knowledge that they're always in control. A popular alternative spot which is exposed to more swell than Langland is Llangennith at the far west of the Gower.

Advanced
The Esp, Porthcawl
A classic break that has everything you could want. It's shallow (very shallow sometimes) when it starts working at about mid to high tide, and it's a reefbreak so beware! The bay consists of a heavy sucky left-hander which breaks to the beach, and a right-hander which is longer but not as hollow, but this needs a big swell to work. The Esp is intense and perfect for mastering airs or tube riding.

Phil Holden

FRESHWATER WEST IN PEMBROKESHIRE, ONE OF WALES'S PRIME LOCATIONS.

North Cornwall

Arguably Britain's best stretch of coastline, the north coast of Cornwall receives the biggest and most consistent surf in the country. With a healthy population of local surf girls there'll be no shortage of inspiration and a great selection of open aspect beaches which pick up any swell from passing lows. Away from the crowded areas of Newquay you can escape to find beachbreaks or reefs to suit most levels.

KAY HOLT BASHES THE TOP OFF A FISTRAL WALL

Beginner
Newquay Bay
The gently-shelving beaches of Towan, Great Western and Tolcarne are sheltered from the brunt of Atlantic swells, so are ideal places for the learner to gain some confidence. They are also offshore on the prevailing southwesterly winds, and although they are not renowned for their quality waves they often provide some good clean faces. Surfing is banned on Towan in the summer. At high tide Tolcarne produces wedgy shorebreak conditions which will take you into the intermediate/ experienced realm.

Intermediate
Fistral
The most famous of the Cornish beaches, Fistral has plenty of lifeguard cover, rolling waves (at anything other than low tide when it breaks hard), and plenty of channels with few rips. The main hazard at this spot is the crowds, especially in summer, and if you stray into bathing area you are likely to be told off a bronzed Aussie-sounding lifeguard (could be worth a try eh?). The ideal wind is south to south easterly, although it's fun on light onshore winds.

Advanced
Constantine
North of Newquay, Constantine offers less crowded surf and a varied array of good waves. There's a wedgey shorebreak at high tide and a semi-sketchy reef to the left of the beach as the tide drops back. Pointing very slightly southwest Constantine benefits from wind with more east in it than Fistral, and is offshore on a northeasterly. Beware of the reef, it quickly becomes shallow and is best left to advanced surfers only. Constantine has a more laidback feel than Newquay, and is one of the few beaches along this coast which has resisted the urge to have a pub or restaurant built on it. If all you require of a beach is a Mr Whippy van, then this place is for you.

CONSTANTINE REEF — ALLURINGLY PERFECT.

South Cornwall

The South Coast has some of the most beautiful scenery in England. The water is often a beautiful blue, the vibe mellow, and there's a craggy coastline made up of many small coves. When there's a low hanging around off the southwest tip of the country get down there and explore.

Alex Willaims

ROBYN DAVIES AT PORTHLEVEN

Beginner
Praa Sands
Praa Sands is the most popular South Coast beachbreak and works on big southwest swell with winds from the north. A good place to head to when the north coast is blown out on a big northwesterly. There's a fast sucky shorey towards neap high tide with manageable 'learner slopes' at other stages of the tide.

Intermediate
Perranuthnoe
Just along the coast, Perranathnoe works under the same conditions as Praa Sands and can also pack a punch on the bigger swells. A heavy wave with some great peaks on the incoming tide. Avoid it towards high tide as it stops work-ing. Often relatively uncrowded.

Advanced
Porthleven
The jewel in the South Coast's crown, this is an excellent reefbreak but unfortunately everybody knows about it. It holds waves up to 12 feet. However you might get lucky during a weekday and score one of the best waves in England without a huge crowd. It works best when there's a low off Biscay and a northeasterly wind. Best from mid to three quarters tide; avoid low tide, when it's dangerously shallow. Experienced surfers only.

Chris Power

A SOUTH COAST REELER.

North Devon

North Devon is a quality surfing destination with Croyde at the epicentre. It's beginning to get crowded due to the regular influx of surfers from the cities. Treat the locals with respect and expect to get the best waves in the winter and you'll love it.

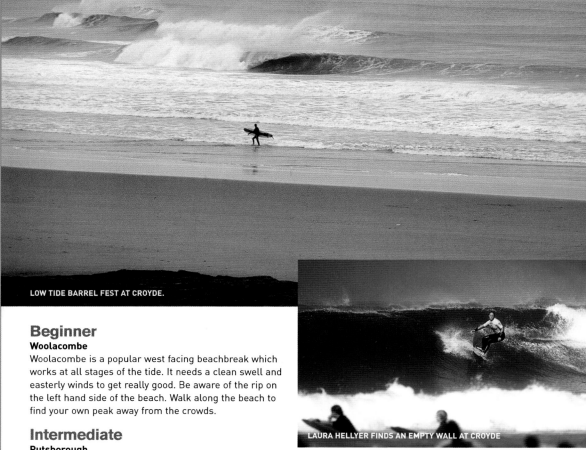

LOW TIDE BARREL FEST AT CROYDE.

LAURA HELLYER FINDS AN EMPTY WALL AT CROYDE

Beginner
Woolacombe
Woolacombe is a popular west facing beachbreak which works at all stages of the tide. It needs a clean swell and easterly winds to get really good. Be aware of the rip on the left hand side of the beach. Walk along the beach to find your own peak away from the crowds.

Intermediate
Putsborough
Situated at the southern end of Woolacombe Bay, this spot works best at high tide. At low tide it drops off, except on very big swells when it gets hollow. It is sheltered on a southwest winds by a high cliff. Good alternative if Croyde is blown out.

Advanced
Croyde
The beachbreak at Croyde works on all tides but is best at low tide when it gets hollow and bowly. Definitely for advanced riders only at low tide over three-foot as the waves break very powerfully and there are some ferocious rips. High tide produces a long peeling wave. Works best on winds from southeast to northeast, with a southwest swell. The reef at Croyde works on a biggish swell, the bowl section can be very intense.

ALex Williams

PUTSBOROUGH — THE SPOT TO CHECK WHEN IT GETS BIG

South Devon

During the winter months the South Coast breaks go off. There are plenty of waves for everyone but when crowds become a problem the adventurous check out some of the secluded reefs. Wait for a low pressure system in the Bay of Biscay and this coast comes to life.

BANTHAM IS OVERLOOKED BY THE ART DECO BURGH ISLAND HOTEL.

Alex Williams

Beginner
Challaborough
The Borough is a consistent mid-to-high tide left hander that picks up a fair amount of swell. A northeast wind is offshore although it is often worth checking on a south or southwesterly as the main peak is sheltered by the cliff. A channel is located directly in front of the car park so the paddle out is relatively easy and duck diving kept to a minimum. The wave itself has a steep enough takeoff but the majority of waves back off before connecting with the inside section.

Intermediate
Bantham Rivermouth
On its day the Rivermouth is a long dredging right hand barrel with frequent sections for hitting the lip. Most of the time though its slack, choppy and rammed with just about anything that will float. The wave is badly affected by anything other than a northeasterly, and is best on the push from low tide onward. Rips are a real hazard at this break especially on an outgoing tide or after heavy rain (when the banks are best due to a build up of sand). On its day Bantham can be a great intermediate wave but it is fickle.

Advanced
Bovisands
The left-hand point at Bovisands is home to one of sharpest and most uneven reefs in Britain, and getting into and out of the lineup can be difficult. There are usually hollow sections but if you fall off you'll hit the bottom as it's ridiculously shallow. Water quality at this break is also poor and it can be crowded as it's so close to Plymouth. If you fancy a real challenge it's one of the gnarliest South Coast reefs. Experts only!!

A SOUTH DEVEON SECRET SPOT.

Dorset

The South Coast might not be the most consistent area for surf in the Britain but when there's a swell pushing up The Channel it can turn it on.

Gary Knights

QUALITY SOUTH COAST WAVES

Beginner
Boscombe Pier

On a high tide in pretty much any wind and with the right swell Boscombe goes off. It provides nice wedgy shorey peaks which can be heavy and hold their shape. Lefts and rights on most southerly swells. The Pier provides shelter from strong south west winds but can be a little crowded at the weekends.

Intermediate
Southbourne

Most of the time it's a mellow beginners to intermediate wave, but on large swell it's a notorious shore dump best left to bodyboarders. It works mainly on a south west swell but easterly swells can produce long, clean rides. On solid swells outer banks begin to work on an old sea wall about 400m from shore. No shelter from SW gales and not for the faint hearted.

Advanced
Secret Spots

There are a cluster of good reefbreaks on the south coast, all of which work on a southwest groundswell with no winds or gentle northerly offshores. The waves break over limestone ledges in very shallow water — not for the inexperienced. These are some of the best breaks on the coast so you can guarentee they'll be crowded in good conditions.

Chris Power

BOURNEMOUTH PIER

Gary Knights

PERFECT SOUTH COAST LEDGES

Jersey

Jersey is the largest of the Channel Islands. During the summer months most surfing is restricted to the west coast – the north and south coasts need big winter swells to work.

A PORTION OF JERSEY JUICE

Dave Ferguson

Beginner
The Watersplash
The Watersplash, known as the 'Splash', is the centre of Jersey surfing, situated in the middle of the five-mile-long west facing St Ouen's Bay. The surf can get very hollow at low tide, but once the tide pushes in, the Splash offers nice easy peeling lefts and rights, giving some good long rides. The Splash is the most consistent spot on the island, and tends to pick up more swell than the surrounding beach breaks to the north and south. There are lifeguards on duty at El Tico, which overlooks the Splash, during the spring and summer months. The Splash is home to the busy Watersplash nightclub, cafe and bars, a great place to hangout after surfing.

Intermediate
Barge Aground
The Barge is the first of the hollow high-tide spots that stretch northwards from Secrets to L'Etacq. There are generally two waves at the Barge, the lefts that break just south of the steps, and the A-frame peak which breaks in front of the boat-shaped house that overlooks the break. The waves at the Barge are first shaped by outer reefs, before they jack up on the inside sandbar providing crisp hollow French-style barrels. The Barge doesn't really hold much size; after about four foot, the sets tend to break on the outer reef and wash all the way through. However the Barge's quality is in the two to three foot range which makes it the perfect summer surf spot.

Advanced
Petit Port
One of Jersey's infamous big-wave reefs, Petit Port comfortably holds 15-foot-plus waves, but also offers good waves from three foot upwards too. Petit Port, situated near the south-west tip of the island, will always be bigger then everywhere else. A four- to five-foot swell hitting the Watersplash can produce six- to eight-foot sets at Petit Port. At high tide there are two peaks, the first one is a short and very shallow breaking peak, which offers sketchy takeoffs followed by good tube rides. The second peak is better at high tide, providing heavy rights up to ten feet. The lefts are ridable too, but tend to break into deeper water. Access is from either the rocks or slipway at the bottom of the hill to Corbiere. Experts only.

THE VIEW OF ST OUENS FROM THE WATERSPLASH PUB

Dave Ferguson

Northeast

As a surf location, Scarborough has many critics. The water is cold nd brown, and the swell are inconsistant. Yet those with a little local knowledge, patience, and a warm wetsuit know the surf here can rival anywhere in the country. Home to reefs, points and beaches, Scarborough has something for all abilities and is home to a surprisingly large surfing population. Autumn is the best time surf here. The surf is more consistent than any other season, and the water isn't too cold.

SOUTH SHIELDS

Beginner
South Bay
This is a good beginner's beachbreak, surfable throughout all stages of the tide, although beginners should be wary of the spa wall at high tide. South Bay often cleans up the surf in big swells, due to the shelter it receives from the harbour, and it's popular when other places are too big and blown out. A good place to learn, but can get crowded at the weekend.

Intermediate
North Bay
This is another good beachbreak which is good for beginners when small. Generally, North Bay is more powerful than South Bay as it is more open to northerly swells. Best at low tide, although for the more experienced there can be a sick shore-break as the tide nears high known as 'Supasucks'. Be cautious when surfing on an incoming tide when surfing the castle end of the bay, as access can be difficult due to the sea defences.

Advanced
Cayton Bay
Situated just outside Scarborough, Cayton Bay is the swell magnet of the area, which in turn means crowds can be a problem during weekends and especially during holidays. Home to three breaks, 'Bunkers' at high tide can offer fast, powerful, hollow barrels. 'Pumphouse' can be surfed throughout all tidal stages, but 'Cayton Point' only works at high tide. This is a very sketchy but sick wave, breaking over boulders which should only be ridden by experienced surfers. It's likely to be crowded when it's working, but can definitely be worth it. When small, Cayton Bay offers good waves for learners; when big it's best left to the experienced as it's probably one of the most powerful waves in the area.

Stu Norton

Scotland

Swells from the Arctic pound the Scottish coastline to produce some of the most powerful surf in Europe. Scotland's east coast can get classic and there's surf on many of the outer islands, but what attracts surfers to Scotland is its infamous North Shore.

Alex Williams

PERFECT WAVES, BEAUTIFUL COUNTRYSIDE AND NOT ANOTHER PERSON IN SIGHT. WELCOME TO SCOTLAND! STRATHY.

Beginner
Aberdeen
There are several peaks here which work best on a south swell but pick up a north swell too. West winds are offshore, but cross shores are okay. The beach is good for beginners and the groynes provide some good fun waves but make sure you don't surf too close!

Intermediate
Thurso East
An excellent tube-riding wave, best surfed at higher tides for intermediates. When it's on, big rights peel endlessly down the reef and into the rivermouth. Fast, heavy waves break over shallow rocks so be aware that if you surf this place over three foot you'll be entering the advanced realm. When the tide gets low it can get gnarly but it's a good reef primer.

Alex Williams

ELOISE TAYLOR CUTS BACK AT BRIMMS NESS

Chris Power

COLD AND REMOTE, BRIMMS NESS HOLDS PERFECT WAVES.

Advanced
Brimms Ness
Brimms is a platform of rock ledges which stick out into the Arctic to form a small point which produces three different waves. 'The Bowl' and 'The Cove' are hollow right handers and work from mid to high tide and 'The Point' is a low tide left which wraps around the rocks at the eastern end. The take off at Brimms is quick and ledgy but the barrel is perfect. All waves break on shallow ledges – for experts only.

Travel zones

Travel is the spice of the surfer's life. It open's your eyes, enriches your heart and broadens your mind. Travel is the surf student's greatest teacher. Go and learn.

the only thing that you can carry with you on your travels is your heart. fill your heart with good things and good things will follow you for the rest of your life Scott Murray - travel writer.

Short haul

'So many waves, so little time', is the often-quoted mantra of the surf traveller. Luckily cheap flights and tailor-made holidays mean that 24 hours after reading this you could be on the other side of the globe having the best surf of your life!

Tara Moller

SARAH BENTLEY, BOILERS, MOROCCO.

Agadir, Morocco

What to expect Deep in the heart of North Africa there is a fishing village called Tarazoute, just north of Agadir which comes alive each winter with the sound of surf banter. It's a beautiful place with rich Arabic cultural differences adding to the magic.

When to go October to April, with December, January and February being the pick of the months.

Where to surf There are several beachbreaks south of Tarazoute suitable for beginners. Intermediates and experts can take advantage of pointbreaks like Boilers and Anchor Point which are suitable for intermediate surfers when small, but can also hold waves big enough to test any expert.

What will £20 buy you? At one of the Souks (local markets) you could get all manner of local trinkets, knitted bags and funky presents for everyone at home.

Portugal

What to expect surprisingly cool water, punchy beachbreaks and some lovely long wrapping points. Portugal's long coast has something for everyone.

When to go The best time of year is March to September.

Where to surf The warm Algarve coast has a great variety of beaches for beginners and some nice waves for advanced surfers. The more rugged reefs of Ericeria produce some challenging conditions for advanced surfers. Peniche has some great waves for beginners and Super Tubos for the advanced surfer. Peniche also has the added advantage of being located on a peninsula so no matter what the wind direction there is usually somewhere to surf.

What will £20 buy you? The Portuguese love to party the coolest Portuguese clubs don't get started until at least 1am. £20 would pay for a night on the tiles. If it's flat, check out Lisbon, it's one of the grandest cities in Europe (Just avoid the roads during rush hour).

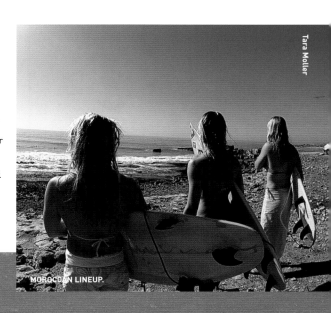

Tara Moller

MOROCCAN LINEUP.

SUPER TUBOS, PORTUGAL

Ricardo Bravo

Board Repairs

ó

top tip

You can get boards repaired in most places these days, but a little tube of Solar Rez, or similar is always useful to have handy. If you have fixed fins take a small ding repair kit and learn how to repair a bust fin, just in case. Always carry a spare leash, leash string, wax, and if you've got fin systems get an extra Allen key or screw driver and spare fins. Put them in a small zip up bag that will sit flat and pack away easily in your board bag.

Short haul

Hossegor, France

What to expect Ten kilometres of the best beachbreaks in the world. Graviere, La Nord, Estagnots and Bourdaines are names that roll off the tongue and stir the blood of surfers in a manner akin to those of Enrique, Farrell and Clooney!

When to go The deep water trench located off the Landes coast sucks every morsel of swell from the Atlantic Ocean and focuses it on the hard shallow sands. March to October is best for swell, but try to hit the area in September when the summer's warmth is still in the air and water, yet the crowds are heading home.

Where to surf Finding the waves is easy, just pick your favourite spot and check it. If it's no good, just choose a direction, north or south, and walk. If the weather and swell patterns are in place, you won't be disappointed. La Estagnots is a favourite, as is Le Penon.

What will £20 buy you? If you do fail in your mission to find waves, head for the roadside coffee bars and then venture forth to the legendary nightspots like the Rock Food or Casino. Just don't plan much surfing the next day! For £20 you'll get a nice meal and two or three beers.

Gary Knights

HOSSEGOR IN THE SUMMER TIME

Chris Power

DESERT ISLAND DIVAS CHECKING A TASTY BREAK IN THE CANARIES.

The Canaries

What to expect Located just far enough south to escape the full bite of the northern hemisphere winter, the Canaries have long been a refuge for the battered European surfer.

When to go From September to March swells pulse down from intense Atlantic storms and unload onto the beaches of the Fortunate Isles. The water is warm, the living cheap, and sunshine is guaranteed.

Where to surf For beginners and intermediates head straight to Famara Beach on Lanzarote, and Flag beach or Cotillo on Fuerteventura. For advanced surfers, the small fishing village of La Santa on Lanzarote is one of the most popular wintering grounds with three world-class breaks. On Fuerteventura head off on the Northern Track in search of waves.

What will £20 buy you? It'll pay for you and a friend to enjoy the best tapas money can buy in one of the cafes in Famara village or it'll almost pay for you to rent a car for the day. Surfgirl run coaching holidays to Lanzarote each winter. Check out www.surfgirlmag.com for more details.

Alex Williams

LANZAROTE SUNSET.

Long haul

Alex Williams

Barbados

Barbados is one of the coolest places to surf. The locals are laid back, the water is turquoise and white sandy beaches are empty. The east coast has heavy breaking waves of excellent quality on their day. The west coast has the most picture perfect scenery and is the holiday destination of Johnny Depp and a whole host of other stars. The south coast offers fun rolling waves and the island enjoys a beautifully tropical climate.

When to go October to January there is consistently good weather and reasonably consistent waves.

ó Packing

top tip

Protection is everything. Buy a good boardbag that can hold all your boards easily. It'll last for ever. Bear in mind the number of boards you're likely to need and that you may want to pack the nose, tail and fins when choosing a bag size. Coffin bags are great and you can always bung loads of stuff in them if you're going over the baggage allowance. (Most airlines won't weigh your surfboards). If you intend to hike a lot try one of the double type bags, they may be easier to carry. The most vulnerable parts of a surfboard are the nose, tail and fins. Foam off cuts (usually available from any shaper) make ideal packing materials if you have fixed fins, or want to pad out nose and tail areas. You can even use the rail off cuts to guard rails. Alternatively try custom shaping some polystyrene. Or try the blow-up fin protectors or bubble wrap. Chuck wetsuits, booties and so on in around the fins filling gaps and providing extra padding. Flip flops or sandals can easily be slipped on the outside of fixed fins or over the back fin to provide extra support during flights. If you have no packing available you could try wrapping duct tape around the fins to secure them as an emergency measure.

Simon Williams

travel safety

"Adversity is usually the result of poor planning, inadequate equipment, incompetence or a combination of the three. One way to avoid adversity is to stay at home. Another way is to learn the skills and acquire the equipment that will make adversity a remote possiblity." Steve England

With ever increasing numbers of surfers in the water and surfers travelling further to score waves, the incidents of injuries and the associated horror stories are rising steadily. Statistically surfing isn't classified as a dangerous sport, but when things get out of control it does get heavy.

Whether you're just travelling down to your local beach or to the jungles of Indonesia it is your responsibility as a surfer to know how to deal with dangerous situations. Shit happens, and it's happening more often. Relying on the knowledge or bravery of others just isn't enough.

Much of this advice may sound basic. It is, but you'd be surprised how many times people ignore the basics and get into trouble. If you 'know before you go' you'll dramatically reduce the chances of it happening to you.

Where to surf Beginners and intermediates should check out Freights, South Point and Silversands. The whole of the west coast is riddled with suitable spots for intermediate level surfers. For advanced level surfers there's Soup Bowl on the east coast and Duppies on the north point of the island.
What will £20 buy you? You'd be able to eat the best fresh fish or a steak whilst enjoying a live band, followed by an evening at The Harbour Lights where you could drink as much as you want! The local yellow buses will take you anywhere for $1.50 while blasting out reggae tunes.

GETTING TUBED IN BARBADOS.

Alex Williams

JEFFREY'S BAY – ONE OF THE WORLD'S FINEST WAVES

Jeffrey's Bay, South Africa

What to expect Africa – just the word conjures up images of adventure. To the surfer, Africa means Durban, Cape Town and one wave in particular: the princess of the south, Jeffrey's Bay. A small town now surrounds this legendary wave that has become a Mecca for surfers around the globe

When to go Best season: April- July, but there are waves all year round in Cape Town and Durban.

Tara Molle

Where to surf Beginners should check out North Beach in Durban for plenty of fun peaks. Intermediates can head for for the shelving waves of Ballito and the Umhlanga Rocks area. Advanced surfers should check out J-Bay. At its best J-Bay is all things to all surfers, a long wave with plenty of room for manoeuvres, tube riding and speed. Cold and often windy (from the storms needed to produce the optimum surf conditions) this is not the place to go to bask on the beach.

What will £20 buy you? The close proximity of the world renowned national wildlife parks, mean lounging around and sunbathing should be low on your list of priorities. £20 will pay for a great day out that you won't forget for a lifetime.

Pete Frieden

ó Take a spare board!

top tip

If you want to surf big waves on your travels make sure you've got a board that can handle the additional power. Get a gun, try it out here to make sure you like the way it paddles and turns. If you have to save up then get on with it now. There is no substitute for the confidence you get from being happy with your equipment when you are paddling for the wave of your life! Travel insurance that covers surfboards is available through the BSA.

California, USA

California boasts some prime surfing spots, more McDonalds than you could visit in a lifetime and more beautiful people than you could ever imagine.
When to go In the winter you'll need a 3mm full suit. In the summer you just need a short sleeve spring suit. The non-wuss can go without a suit during July and August. Winter's probably the best. La Jolla really ropes in the swell and there's snow in the mountains. The weather is super nice, lots of sun with the temperature getting up to 20°C.
Where to surf Beginner and intermediate surfers could battle the crowds at beachbreaks such as

CALIFORNIA DREAMIN'.

David Pulu

Huntington Beach. Advanced surfers should head for the numerous reefbreaks of La Jolla and one of the best beachbreaks – Black's.
What will £20 buy you? About ten gut-plugging Burritos, eight McDonald's cheeseburgers, two CD's, enough petrol to drive to the mountains and back in the winter to go snowboarding, or petrol and insurance for a day trip into Mexico for a surf.

• **Know your ability, strengths and weaknesses.** If you're going out into surf that it out of your league you are threatening not only your own life, but those of other surfers and those of the people who may have to come and rescue you. Everyone has their limits; to stretch them too far isn't cool, it's stupid.

• **CPR** If you're thinking of going further than a two week package holiday to the Canaries or are going out into large or remote surf you should know ocean rescue and more serious first aid like CPR. Even if you don't intend to go to Jaws it's still a good idea to take a course. You never know when it may come in useful.

• **Check travel insurance**, and if you're travelling anywhere remote get helicopter evacuation cover. Keep these details safe and easily accessible along with emergency contact numbers.

• **If you're going to remote areas** make sure you and your friends know an established emergency procedure, ie find out where the nearest medical centre or hospital is, and check it's contact numbers. Even if its three days travel away at least you'll have a plan and be able to act on it instead of wandering around lost and in shock.

• **If you're out in the bush**, check your position on a decent map. Store grid reference numbers of your position in case of heli evacuation. Maybe even write them down and post them in the surf camp so everyone knows.

• **Carry a mobile.** Most countries and areas are covered by satellite mobile networks these days. A couple of years ago a girl marooned in the Lombok text messaged her boyfriend in Perranporth to get help. It worked, all were saved.

Long haul

6 Checking in

Always be polite to the check in folk as they have the ability to make your life hell. When checking boards in at the airport always ask if they are going as part of your luggage allowance because they're so light. Most airline companies in the UK have cottoned on to the fact that they can make a bit of extra cash from surfers carrying boards and will charge to take them. Always check the cost before you book your ticket. If you suspect your board to be damaged when you arrive at the airport after a flight check it immediately and report any damage to the representatives. Most airlines require that you sign an indemnity form these days, but that shouldn't excuse them from negligent damage.

top tip

The North Shore, Oahu, Hawaii

What to expect This ten-mile stretch of coast contains some of the best surf spots on earth. Pipeline, Sunset, and Wiamea Bay are the places where legends have been created and reputations crushed. Huge swells derived from north Pacific storms radiate down and slam into the volcanic island chain, producing surf that is larger and more powerful than anywhere else on earth. It's where the final leg of the men's pro tour comes to town to crown its World Champion at the Banzai Pipeline, a gladiator pit that breaks just metres from the shore. On land the atmosphere is almost as electric as in the ocean.

When to go From November to March.

Where to surf For beginners and intermediates it tends to be spectating only, apart for the really small days when Ehukai Beach park is fun. Also check out Monster Mush or V-Land when the swell is small and managable.

What will $20 buy you? It'll buy two of you breakfast in the Cafe Halewia and you'll hear all about that mornings exploits straight from the horses mouths; the heroics, the performances, the horror stories. Although the surf only occasionally gets small enough for mere mortals to head out, every surfer must come here at least once in their lifetime; if not to surf, then just to savour the atmosphere and watch the spectacle.

Joli

MALIA JONES, ROCKY POINT

Western Australia

What to expect This pristine coastline, backed by harsh desert, offers plenty of room to explore some of the world's best waves. From the desert camps of The Bluff and Gnaraloo to the surfing/ fishing town of Margaret River, the WA experience is most definitely a rootsy affair. One of the world's great surf adventures.
When to go March - June.
Where to surf Beginners should head for Cottesloe Beach in the Perth area; there's a whole variety of shapely peaks ideal for all ability levels. Intermediates should check out Scarborough Beach for a few barrels.

Gold Coast, Australia

What to expect The pointbreaks of Kirra, Burleigh Heads and Greenmount on Australia's Gold Coast have been described as the surfing world's great natural wonders. If you want to enjoy them at their best though you'll have to set your alarm clock, as the coast has now taken over from Malibu as one of the most crowded surf spots on earth. If you move onto the numerous beaches however you'll find plenty of room. And if it goes flat, well, this is Australia's richest holiday destination so there's plenty more to do.
When to go January to April is generally the best time to visit the Gold Coast.
Where to surf Beginners and intermediates just pick a beach. There are miles and miles of beaches suitable for learning. For advanced the surfers, Snapper super-bank stretching from Snapper Rocks, through Rainbow Bay to Kirra is now world famous, but crowded. Burleigh Heads and Currumbin offer great alternatives.
What will £20 buy you? From sports fishing to the multiplex cinemas, bars, nightclubs, golf courses and the most varied selection of restaurants found anywhere in the world, there's plenty to spend your money on. £20 will get you entry into the cinema followed by a light snack at Sushi Train afterwards.

TRUDY TODD BLASTS OFF THE TOP AT HOME IN QUEENSLAND'S TROPICAL WATERS.

ROCHELLE BALLARD, HAWAII.

Joli

Long haul

SAM CORNISH, SLOTTED IN INDONESIA.

Simon Williams

Simon Williams

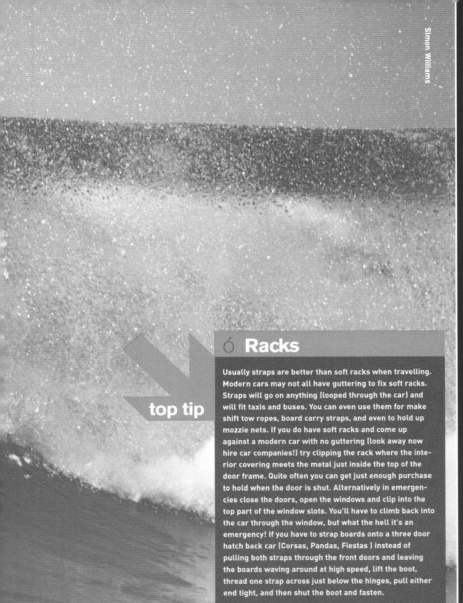

Simon Williams

Tara Moller

ó Racks

top tip

Usually straps are better than soft racks when travelling. Modern cars may not all have guttering to fix soft racks. Straps will go on anything (looped through the car) and will fit taxis and buses. You can even use them for make shift tow ropes, board carry straps, and even to hold up mozzie nets. If you do have soft racks and come up against a modern car with no guttering (look away now hire car companies!) try clipping the rack where the interior covering meets the metal just inside the top of the door frame. Quite often you can get just enough purchase to hold when the door is shut. Alternatively in emergencies close the doors, open the windows and clip into the top part of the window slots. You'll have to climb back into the car through the window, but what the hell it's an emergency! If you have to strap boards onto a three door hatch back car (Corsas, Pandas, Fiestas) instead of pulling both straps through the front doors and leaving the boards waving around at high speed, lift the boot, thread one strap across just below the hinges, pull either end tight, and then shut the boot and fasten.

Preparing for your big trip!

A basic travel check list:
Boards. Do you have the right board(s) for the conditions you'll face?
Do you need wetsuits or rash vests? Always take two pairs of boardies just in case one pair rips.
Reef boots. They look silly but so does sitting on the beach with reef cuts when the waves are firing.
Spare leashes, and leash string.
Do you have the right wax for the region's water temperature?
Have you got a good boardbag to protect your sticks?
Have you packed them correctly?
Do you need spare fins, or fin keys?
Travel straps or racks for taxis, hire cars, buses.
Do you need a ding kit or will Solar Rez do?
Duck tape for packing and sealing dings.
Vaseline for rubs.
Sunscreen, total block and Aloe aftersun.
Tea tree oil - for bites and cuts.
Insect repellent - 100% jungle formula Deet works on body and bed clothes
TRavel Insurance – make sure your details can be easily found by your travel partners so evacuation can be easily and quickly organised.

Bali, Indonesia

What to expect There are many perfect waves within the archipelago of Indonesia that could make this list but Bali is still the Island of the God's. Despite the horrific bombing of Kuta in 2003 the island is still a very special place. The hospitality of the people, beauty of the countryside and perfect waves make it a magical place. Even though most of the waves break over sharp shallow coral reefs there are a number of breaks suitable for beginners and intermediates. Those that make the pilgrimage will be rewarded by memories that will last a lifetime.
When to go May to November is the dry season when the waves seem to be offshore everyday and it never rains. All year round you can score waves there though.
Where to surf Beginners – Kuta and Legian Beaches offer great waves for learning, but watch out for rips. Intermediates – Dreamland and Cangu offer more of a challenge with long rivermouth waves of Medawai offering an adventure. Advanced – Uluwatu, Padang Padang, Bingin, Nusa Dua, Sanur - take your pick!
What will £20 buy you? Twenty sarongs, four slap-up meals or you could get your hair platted and your nails painted everyday for a week!

Party places

Here's SurfGirl's guide to the best party hotspots in Europe.

Arrecife Carnival, Lanzarote, February - March.
Leave your English reserve behind and get Latin for a while at the Arrecife Carnival. The entire seafront and nightclub area is fenced off for a week and turned into a nocturnal amusement park. Thousands of people in fancy dress gyrating to non-stop salsa bands, cheap and strong Cuba Libres (rum and coke), surfers stumbling about, the odd surf star, parades that look like they've just come from Rio, all thrown together in a fragrant and volatile mix that can be so much fun that it can only possibly happen once a year. Plus it's still peak surf season, so you can fill both your days and nights with pleasure.

The Casino, Hossegor, July - September.
This is a casino and nightclub only a ten minute-stumble from the main bars in Hossegor. In prime surf season The Casino is always packed with pro's trying to look like James Bond, wannabees, and the lowly blind-drunk surfer. The admission fee is nothing compared to the prices at the bar. There's a fenced-off well-guarded outdoor pool which shines like a beacon of hope amongst the chaos. The large sign telling you that bathing is not allowed beckons anyone with a modicum of mischief to bathe in its cleansing waters. The idea is to enter the pool, and evade capture for as long as possible. The record for speedy eviction is three minutes from door-queue-to-pool and back to the door set by a group of bodyboarders from Plymouth.

Rip Curl Boardmasters, Newquay - early August.
Newquay – you either love it or you hate it, but for one week of the year it'd be hard not to have fun...if you're a party animal. Now labelled Britain's 'Ibiza' the town is absolutely packed and when the pro's arrive in town it goes ballistic. Week-long party binges, people waking up in fields, supermarket trolley racing, cave parties, beach parties and no end of mischief are all common distractions weakening the knees of the pro surf hopefuls. All you have to do is rock up and join in!

La Triangu, Bilbao, Basque country - mid August.
As most seasoned travellers may already know, the Basques are a very quiet and reserved people. They can hardly ever be seen enjoying themselves, hanging out in bars, having week-long outrageous parties, drinking kalimotxo, dancing in the street or being chased by bulls. Mid August is "La Semana Grande", the Fiestas of Bilbao. Obviously everybody will be too busy working to go out, apart from the odd game of bingo of course. The coolest bar to hang out around here is called La Triangu, just up the road from the Iranian Embassy beach. Good music, nice garden, live bands, perfect for young and old surfers alike.

The SAS Ball, Cornwall - early September.
With 3,500 surfers and chicks dressed up to the eyeballs, drinking, dancing, and partying till dawn it's one of a kind hedonism has drawn praise from celebs, studs and hardened night crawlers. The Darkness, Faithless, and Dreadzone have all played. You have to be an SAS member and tickets sell out months in advance. We always crack on about it, but we haven't seen anything like it anywhere.

Lisbon's nightclubs, Portugal - all year.
It's little known fact that Lisbon has some of the best dance clubs in Europe. The locals have an amazing propensity to go out and dance all night without the need to get absolutely legless. Has to be seen to be believed we know, but once you've seen the locals dancing on tables until sunrise you may be persuaded that there is an alternative the good old British 'lash it up and fall over before closing time' routine.

If you fancy chillin' with a nice cool beer after a hard day's surf, here's some tried and tested venues for you to check out.

The Watersplash, Jersey
If you're heading for Jersey then look no further than the St Ouens beach-front bar, The Watersplash. A renowned surfer's watering hole since its establishment, and host to some legendary performances, the bar has morphed itself into a big rave-(wave)-style club. This coupled with it's location make it the club for visiting surfers to experiencet!

The Bootleggers Bar, Bundoran, Ireland
The Bootleggers on Bundoran's main street is one of the best live venues in the northwest. If you're there on a Wednesday night check out the local band Box-T. The whole place wil be jumping!

The Thatch, Croyde
A picturesque Devonshire cottage on the outside, raging bar on the inside. The Thatch is a really cool pub with excellent food, bands and most of Croyde Suf Club propping up the bar on any given night.

The Extreme Acadamy, Watergate Bay, Newquay.
A really cool bar right on the beach at Watergate Bay. Lovely food and amazing views. Perfect!

The King's Head, Gower
After a hard day's surfing at Llangennith pop into the The Kings Head, a lively summer time pub. If the surf has been good it'll be packed with stoked surfers.

good books

If you're going travelling it's wise to be armed with as much information as possible. Here's SurfGirl's selection of travel books that cover most surfing destinations around the world. And, if you're airport bound or suffering from flat surf syndrome, there's also some suggested reading for your entertainment.

travel guides

The Stormrider Guide
The Stormrider guidebooks are great. Informative and well designed, they're packed with details on numerous surf breaks, with maps and photos to give you a good visual awareness of your chosen destination. There's three books in the series – Europe, North America and the World – which should just about cover any trip your planning. **£24.94.**

Big Blue Surf Guide – Spain
This is the only English language surf guide entirely dedicated to Spain, and it certainly deals with its chosen subject area in great depth. Pretty much every possible spot is divulged in detail. This book serves the same purpose as both a Rough Guide and a surf guide, and because of its superb practical qualities it'll definitely be one of the first things to be packed during a surf trip to Spain. **£16.99**

Portugal
Penned by Stuart Butler this is the only surf guide devoted solely to Portugal, with all the essential information for a killer surf trip. Hundreds of breaks are covered, along with advice on ideal swells, winds and tides, as well as practical info on accommodation, food and nightlife. **£10.99**

Surfing in South Africa
A complete guide to surfing in South Africa. Detailed surf spot profiles from the northwest coast right around to the Durban coast, including swell prediction, local slang, history and classic surf stories. **£13.50**

Surfing Indonesia
Essential reading for Indo travellers. A compilation of surf break summaries for all Indo regions. Maps, photos, lingo, equipment and loads of useful info for the travelling surfer. **£12.95**

Surfing Australia
From the publishers of Surfing Indonesia. 332 pages of information on breaks, practicalities and accommodation, written by some of Australia's most respected surfers. Maps, info and killer photos in a top quality, easy to carry format. Comprehensive travel guide. **£12.95**

useful

Surfer's Start Up
A comprehensive beginner's handbook which covers all the stuff you need to know. **£9.00**

Longboarder's Start Up
Takes you from the basic skills through to classic nose-riding and progressive manoeuvres. **£9.00**

Surfboard
Fully illustrated instruction manual covering surfboard construction. Learn how to design, shape, glass and repair boards with detailed photos and illustrations. **£14.99**

The Ding Repair Scriptures
How to fix your board. Includes dings, slashes, fins and breaks. A cult classic full of top tips. **£7.00**

interest

Pipe Dreams
If you ever wanted to know about Kelly Slater's life and what makes him tick, then this is the book for you. His autobiography covers the formative years spent around Cocoa Beach, moves on to his life as the world's greatest competitive surfer, and shows us glimpses into his private life. It gives us a fascinating insight into the mind of one of the sport's most successful athletes, and although it doesn't dish the dirt as much as we'd like, it's still very compelling reading. **£18.99**

MP. The Life of Michael Peterson
MP was one of the greatest surfers the world has ever seen in the 70's. He was worshipped like a god – other surfers got out of the water to watch him, and girls threw themselves at him. Then he imploded into a world of hard drugs, fast cars and shadows. He eventually hit rock bottom after a car chase involving 35 police cars and after years of jail and psychiatric institutions he emerged alive, but bearing the scars of battle. Michael Peterson was a tortured genius...and one complex cat!

Surfers
In *Surfers* writer Matt Griggs gives an insider's view of a line up of surfing's most interesting and unique characters, 26 in all from Ozzie Wright to Occy and Mick Fanning. At turns funny and sad but always inspiring, this book lifts the lid on one of the world's most dynamic, enigmatic and mysterious sports. **£14.99**

All these books and many more are available from our online shop at www.orcasurf.co.uk

Surfing
and
relationships

Surfing is a passionate sport and is often a source of conflict between surfers and their partners, the 'third person' in the relationship. Here Lauren McCrossan explains her experience of combining a relationship with surfing, and how she was able to successfully reconcile the two.

"GABE, COME IN YOUR TIME IS UP, I'M COLD, BORED AND STARVING!"

Sylvain Cazenave

Having been introduced to surfing some eight years ago, I have come to realise that a dinosaur-sized bone of contention between surfers and their non-surfing partners is the person in the relationship who does not understand the pull of the ocean. Undoubtedly the problem is a real one. I have met countless partners of dedicated surfers who groan when their man starts waxing his board, who moan about coming second in his list of priorities after the ocean...and his surfing mates... and his boards...and the tides... (okay make that fifth on his list of priorities) and who dream of the day when he books them a romantic city break in Prague, rather than two weeks in a van in Hossegor. Then again, do surfers do enough to explain their need to don a wetsuit, booties and incredibly unflattering hood and paddle out on a rain-lashed beach in the middle of

December in the name of fun? Do surfers really expect your average girlfriend on the street to understand why this might be more enjoyable than wandering around a heated shopping mall or cuddling up on the sofa with a glass of wine and the EastEnders omnibus?

At this stage I must point out that with the strong emergence of women's surfing especially over the last few years, there will be many cases where it is the boyfriend of a surfing girl who is trying to drag her away from checking weather charts and planning surf trips. So despite the fact that I am going to explore this from the point of view of being the girlfriend or wife of a surfer, please interpret this to fit your own circumstances (deleting he or she as appropriate!).

When I first met my husband, Gabriel Davies, a Quiksilver

Alex Lloyd

surfing such places as Hawaii and Southwest France and, being a professional as he is, I have to admit (obvious bias aside) that he is a joy to watch. I do wonder, though, about the girls who are forced to sit for hours watching their partner floundering around and only occasionally clambering to his feet, or going over the falls every set as he desperately tries to perfect duck-diving. And obviously it is a disappointing come-down when you do have that great surf (no matter what your capabilities) only to paddle in and be greeted by a face thunderous enough to create the fifty year storm but I believe this is where the old adage, however corny, comes into play that 'only a surfer knows the feeling'.

I have come to realise these words ring very true. Surfing is not just a hobby; it is an all-encompassing addictive passion. It is not like playing golf or being part of a Sunday League football team. Surfing is dependent on the ocean, on nature, so it is much more complex than booking a tee-time and knowing that the golf course will be exactly as you left it the last day you played. Surfing is complex in this way because it is more difficult to predict where and when that perfect swell will hit. It is difficult to commit yourself to, for example, a romantic weekend in the Lake District or your partner's friend's wedding so far in advance, if you don't know whether that commitment will fall on the one day of perfect waves for months. Therein, I think, lies the cause of much frustration for a couple where only one party is a surfer and the reason why many partners feel that they are not the first priority because, in many ways, they are not. If a pro surfer has to be in the right spot at the right time to get that photograph or to surf that wave then it is very hard to

professional surfer, I'd never seen surfing other than on television and in the delightfully Hollywood *Point Break*, I'd never heard of Kelly Slater, I didn't know how waves were formed and what a surfing manoeuvre was. In fact, I had never even swum in the sea other than dipping my feet in it perhaps once or twice at the age of about six on a family day out to Bournemouth. The first thing I realised, however, when I came into contact with the surfing community was that surfers were simply gobsmacked when I admitted my lack of knowledge. 'But you must have heard of so-and-so?' they would gasp. 'What do you mean you've never been on a surfboard?'

Many surfers, I have come to realise, become so engrossed in what is clearly a wonderful and rewarding pursuit that they forget that time when they did not know all the terminology, or when they hadn't yet stood up on a board and so didn't have endless 'my best waves over the last ten years' stories to recount to other blinkered surfers who also 'know the feeling'. I also remember when a surfer I hardly knew telling me that I should sit with his girlfriend to keep her happy, while he went surfing with my boyfriend, because 'she didn't understand' him. So undoubtedly I had my moments when I wondered what the hell I was doing and what life was like back in the normal world where weather patterns only mattered when you were planning what to wear to go shopping for the afternoon.

You see, because of my introduction to the sport as a complete surfing virgin I do sympathise with partners of surfers. I especially sympathise with those partners of surfers who either only surf in cold places or who, to put it as tactfully as I can, simply aren't very good! I was spared much of this trauma because my husband spends probably half the year

> The first thing I realised, however, when I came into contact with the surfing community was that surfers were simply gobsmacked when I admitted my lack of knowledge. 'But you must have heard of so-and-so?' they would gasp. **'What do you mean you've never been on a surfboard?'**

commit oneself to things going on out there in the non-surfing world. It is generally not just because the surfer is being difficult or selfish (although I am not saying this doesn't happen!) it is just that surfing is different from most other sports and hobbies, being as it is dictated to by tides and winds and weather patterns.

Over time I learned about these factors, which make surfing unique and which non-surfers do not understand and I also learned to identify with the passion that draws people into the lifestyle. I was lucky, I think, in that I had been brought up in a family passionate about sport. We were all racing cyclists and our house was full of bikes, bits of bikes, and libraries of videos featuring the Tour de France and other such events. This background clearly helped me to understand why surfers could be so single-minded about their sport. Needless to say, it was essential for me to understand because surfing is my husband's career, his whole life, not just his weekend pastime. I therefore slipped into the life easily but I still do not think I really

**LAUREN ESCAPING THE SURFER'S
GIRLFRIEND FATE OF THE CAR PARK 'PEN'.**

understood the force which would motivate someone to paddle out in the bitter chill of the Northeast of England with only 5mm of neoprene for protection until I had tried it for myself (surfing that is, not the bitter chill of the Northeast part – I thought I could safely leave that to him!).

The day I suddenly realised that I was standing up on every wave I caught, **I felt a surge of adrenalin and pride rush through me.** The day I managed my first ever cutback, I nearly spontaneously combusted with sheer joy and floated around for at least a day on a cloud of euphoria. It took a few years admittedly, but I am well and truly hooked and now I know how good that feeling is.

Unlike those surfers who say they were hooked from the very first moment they lay on a surfboard and paddled for a wave, I have to admit that it took me a lot longer than that to catch the bug, (although I did catch a few bugs here and there while forcing myself to be dedicated and paddling out in cold, dirty water). My first ever attempt involved donning a man's wetsuit several sizes too big, paddling out on my husband's professional 6'1" that has all the buoyancy of a prawn cracker and bravely swallowing my fear of the ocean and any wave

larger than a two-inch ripple. I was terrified but calmed by my husband's reassuring words about how much fun it was going to be. With his help, I got out to about waist-height water where I lay on the board and prepared for my first wave. I was going to be a surfer. I was going to know what it felt like to catch a wave.

Unfortunately, the second I was pushed into the whitewater, my husband's own board catapulted itself from his side and smacked me square on the top of the head. I eventually emerged bedraggled, a little concussed and completely confused as to how this could ever be a driving force in one's life.

However, mishaps aside, I persevered. Eventually I got my own board and my own properly fitting wetsuit, and after a year or so (I was not, I have to say, a natural Lisa Andersen type) I stood up. It wasn't long after that when I realised I had in fact caught the bug. I realised as I climbed over a sand-dune in France to check the surf, and ran back whooping with delight when I saw a perfect peeling three-foot (well, small-wave riding is an art form too you know!) left-hander. I suddenly heard myself talking about my waves and boring my husband with my after-surf post mortem. The day I suddenly realised that I was standing up on every wave I caught, I felt a surge of adrenalin and pride rush through me. The day I managed my first ever cutback, I nearly spontaneously combusted with sheer joy and floated around for at least a day on a cloud of euphoria. It took a few years admittedly, but I am well and truly hooked and now I know how good that feeling is.

Of course, not every partner of a surfer will want to take up the sport themselves but from my own experience I can definitely recommend it. I love surfing now, regardless of the fact that I am and will never be anywhere near as good as my husband. Also those other little bones of contention about surfing being more a life-changing phenomenon than a mere sport and about every holiday being a surf trip rather than a sight-seeing/lie by the pool/shopping break can also be fantastic advantages rather than disadvantages if you let them. I have made so many friends in the surfing community and one joy of this is that everywhere we go we meet friends and acquaintances we have made through surfing. Even on our honeymoon in the Maldives we bumped into surfers we knew within ten minutes of being on our island and then spent a wonderful fortnight surfing great waves and making even more friends who we will undoubtedly encounter somewhere around the world in the future.

To look back on my complete lack of surfing knowledge eight years down the line is amusing. Not that I am now a surfing oracle but surfing has, through my husband, become an intrinsic part of my life. Almost everywhere we go is dictated to by waves, a large majority of my friends are part of the surfing world and I surf myself. I gave up a career in Law to travel the world with my husband when the surfing lifestyle bug took hold so strongly that I realised I did not want to be sitting in an office

in London when I could be on a beach somewhere riding a board rather than having meetings with the Board. I am now an author and often write my books on the beach, which is a definite improvement to the career I had before. Through surfing I have been to places I would never otherwise have been and met so many people who share the same love of the sport. For my husband and I, surfing is a business but it is also a joy and will always remain a passion.

So, surfers, when you hear yourself complaining about your partner not understanding you, just ask yourself whether

> After all, one thing I can say with 100 percent certitude, that surfer of yours is never going to give it up. They are hooked for life so, as the old saying goes, **if you can't beat them, join them.**

you have done enough to explain that force drawing you into the ocean, or whether you have done enough to make surfing fun for them rather than just leaving them on a cold beach to watch you perform. And non-surfers, if you are perhaps reading this while stuck in that car, peering through the windscreen wipers just to catch a glimpse of him (or her) going over the falls again, ask yourself whether you have done enough to understand the passion and whether in fact you are missing out by not getting out there and having a go for yourself. After all, one thing I can say with 100 percent certitude, that surfer of yours is never going to give it up. They are hooked for life so, as the old saying goes, if you can't beat them, join them.

Alex Williams

OUT OF THE WATER AND IN TO THE...KITCHEN! OH WELL, YOU CAN'T WIN THEM ALL.

TRU LOV

Glossary

Here's some useful surf terms to impress your mates down the beach with.

GNARLY

Aerial An explosive manoeuvre where the surfer launches himself into the air, off the top of the wave.

Barrel A tubular section of a wave within which a surfer can find the meaning of life.

Backhand To ride with your back to the wave.

Beachbreak Waves that break over a sandy bottom, ideal for beginners.

Bottom turn Having dropping down the face of the wave, this is the first turn a surfer uses to set up the next move.

Closeout A wave which breaks along its length all at once, without peeling. Also known as a straight-hander.

CARVE A cool surf mag. Also a powerful turn that throws up loads of spray.

Cutback A manoeuvre performed on the shoulder of the wave that turns the surfer back toward the pocket.

Duck dive The method used by a surfer to push his or her board under an oncoming wave while paddling out.

Drop in When a surfer takes off on a wave that someone else is already riding; a serious breach of surfing etiquette. Remember: the surfer nearest the curl has right of way.

Ding A hole in your surfboard. Often the result of dropping in!

Forehand To ride facing the wave.

Floater A manoeuvre where the surfer rides over the breaking section of the wave and free-falls down the wave's curtain.

Filthy Extremely good.

Glassy Clean, smooth surf conditions when there is no wind.

Gnarly An evil mutha of a wave, intent on destruction; evil conditions.

Goofyfoot A surfer who rides right-foot-forward.

Going off! When the waves are really good, or someone's ripping.

Grommet A young surfer with no respect for his elders, usually in need of some severe discipline!

Groundswell A swell caused by a low pressure system quite a way offshore.

Gun A long, narrow surfboard designed for riding big waves.

Impact zone The area where the waves break.

Kook An idiot who has no idea what he or she is doing.

Left-hander A wave that breaks towards the left as seen from the lineup.

Lineup The area where waves jack up before they break, where surfers wait.

Alex Williams

BARREL - TRUDY TODD.

beautiful images from around the world

The WAVE - Teahupoo - Photography : TIM M^C KENNA

BOTTOM TURN - LAURINA MCGRATH.

Local Someone who surfs a spot regularly, and enjoys moaning on and on about crowds.

Mal Traditional style surfboard around nine feet in length. Hang ten dude!

Natural foot A surfer who rides left-foot-forward.

Nailed To get hammered by the lip of a big wave.

Offshore When the wind blows from the land to the sea, holding up the waves. The ideal wind for surfing.

Onshore The exact opposite. Time to head down the pub!

Over the falls The worst kind of wipeout, when you get dragged down stuck in the lip of the wave.

Pointbreak A rock headland around which waves peel, either to the left or right.

Pumping When the surf is going off. Head for the beach!

Pocket The part of the wave just in front of the curl, where it's steepest.

Quiver A selection of surfboards to suit different conditions.

Rails The edges of a surfboard.

Reefbreak A wave that breaks out to sea, over a slab of rock or coral. Not suitable for beginners.

Rip A dangerous current that can pull you out to sea. If you get caught in one, don't panic, but paddle across it to where the waves are breaking.

Righthander A wave that breaks towards the right, as seen from the lineup.

Rhino chaser A really big board designed for charging huge waves.

Rocker The bottom curve along the length of a surfboard.

Set A group of larger waves which come in periodically.

Sick Very good.

Shorebreak Where waves break close to the sand at a steep beach.

Shoulder The sloping unbroken part of the wave ahead of the pocket.

Soup The whitewater where a wave has just broken. Also a nice hot liquid to be consumed in large quantities after a winter session.

Tube The same as a barrel.

Wipeout See picture below!

Zoo A badly crowded lineup.

WIPEOUT - CHELSEA GEORGESON.